CARNIVAL EVENING

CARNIVAL EVENING

◆

NEW AND SELECTED POEMS:
1968–1998

◆

Linda Pastan

W. W. NORTON & COMPANY

NEW YORK / LONDON

For information about permission to reproduce selections from this book,
write to Permissions, W. W. Norton & Company, Inc.,
500 Fifth Avenue, New York, NY 10110

The text of this book is composed in New Caledonia
with the display set in New Caledonia
Desktop composition by Roberta Flechner
Manufacturing by The Courier Companies, Inc.
Book design by JAM Design

Library of Congress Cataloging-in-Publication Data

Pastan, Linda, 1932–
Carnival evening : new and selected poems, 1968–1998 / by Linda Pastan.
p. cm.
Includes index
ISBN 0-393-04631-1
I. Title.
PS3566.A775C37 1998
813'.54—dc21   97-39860
CIP

W. W. Norton & Company, Inc. 500 Fifth Avenue, New York, N.Y. 10110
http://www.wwnorton.com

W. W. Norton & Company Ltd., 10 Coptic Street, London WC1A 1PU

1 2 3 4 5 6 7 8 9 0

FOR IRA

AND FOR BESS AND JAMIE

Contents

ASPECTS OF EVE, 1975

Acknowledgments

I would like to thank the following places where the work in *New Poems* has appeared:

The Alaska Quarterly Review; The Atlantic Monthly; The Georgia Review; The Gettysburg Review; I've Always Meant to Tell You: Letters to Our Mothers; The New Republic; The Paris Review; Poetry; Poetry International; Prairie Schooner; Shenendoah; The Threepenny Review; Tikkun; Tri Quarterly; Vision; Witness

NEW POEMS,
1998

◆

The Almanac of Last Things

From the almanac of last things
I choose the spider lily
for the grace of its brief
blossom, though I myself
fear brevity,

but I choose *The Song of Songs*
because the flesh
of those pomegranates
has survived
all the frost of dogma.

I choose January with its chill
lessons of patience and despair—and
August, too sun-struck for lessons.
I choose a thimbleful of red wine
to make my heart race,

then another to help me
sleep. From the almanac
of last things I choose you,
as I have done before.
And I choose evening

because the light clinging
to the window
is at its most reflective
just as it is ready
to go out.

Nocturnal

If animals think
about death,
do the nocturnal ones—
the lemur, for instance
or the raccoon—
consider it
a kind of light,
a glare
in the future, a place
where predators
arm themselves in God's
fluorescent shield?

Do they fear
a wilderness of light
the way we fear
the dark? I sleep
with lights burning
in the other room,
as if to fool
what lies ahead, owl-shaped
or prescient
as a bat, waiting
to smother me
in its nocturnal wings.

Le Sens de la Nuit

Magritte, oil on canvas, 1927

Here are some clues
to The Meaning of Night:
pieces of bright foam estranged
from the sea; a woman wrapped
in a cage of winglike shapes;
the formal back of one man twinned
to the front of another—
or are they really the same man,
and could he be the undertaker of day?

If there is a meaning to night
is it contained here, or must we search
through the dreams that lap
behind our closed lids as we sleep
like the small waves in this painting
which, when the day is over
and the museum shuts down,
go back to the dark sea
they came from?

Dreaming of Rural America

Dreaming of rural America,
I want to unbuild my city
brick by brick, dismantling
sidewalks and smokestacks
and subways. I want
to rush to the airport where planes
line up at their gates
like cows at their stalls for milking.
And taking the first plane out,
I want to enter the ticking heart
of the country and in a rented car
drive for miles past fields scored
with the history of wind; past
silos, those inland lighthouses,
where corn smolders to golden dust.
I want an RD number and a tin mailbox
filled with flowers instead of letters.
I want to bathe in a porcelain tub
under a ceiling sloping towards heaven,
and farmyard smells will drift
through the window like notes
of pungent country music.
When I am scrubbed clean,
let a child who has searched
the barn for the perfect egg
offer it to me on her open palm
as if it were the gift of a jewel
on a velvet cushion. In the dream
of rural America, farmers have lost
the knack of despair. They do not
breathe the diesel fumes of whiskey
into the faces of their women.
They do not wield their leather belts
to erase, on the backs of their sons,
the old stigmata of failure.

And on frozen nights no daughter,
dreaming of cities, leans
out of her window to cast wishes
heavy as iron horseshoes towards
the prong of an impossible star.

1936, Upstate New York

In rural America, or the country
as we called it, we rented a room
for the summer in the Schmidt's farmhouse
with flowered curtains at the shiny windows
and spotless, tilting wooden floors.
And the smell of cow drifted through
our room like sweet smoke,
and every morning I helped
to gather eggs, pale as seashells
from their nests in the barn.
At night through the walls

the muffled sounds of German
came from a staticky radio,
and each noon the tin mailbox waited
to be filled—a hungry mouth,
its red flag upright in stiff salute.
I drank milk straight from the pail,
my top lip mustached in creamy white,
and when my mother saw the swastika
on an envelope on the kitchen table,
she packed up fast, and we returned
to the steamy city.

The News of the World

Like weather, the news
is always changing and always
the same. On a map
of intractable borders
armies ebb and flow.
In Iowa a roof is lifted
from its house like a top hat

caught in a swirl of wind.
Quadruplets in Akron.
In Vilnius a radish
weighing 50 pounds.
And somewhere
another city falls
to its knees.

See how the newsprint
comes off on our once
immaculate hands
as we wrap the orange peel
in the sports page
or fold into the comics
a dead bird

the children found
and will bury
as if it were the single
sparrow whose fall
God once promised
to note, if only
on the last page.

October Catechisms

1.

Pilgrim leaves
crowd the air
with their falling
every October.
The journey is always
the same.

2.

Before he is tackled
and the ball bounces free,
there is one moment
when pure exhilaration
feels almost like prayer,
even to a boy.

3.

If we accept the beauty
of the earth and its trees
as a given,
are the cold planets
with their pock-marked faces
early mistakes?

4.

The ritual sadness
of the season
is more voluptuous
than joy.

5.

The animals don't
ask for mercy.
Is it ignorance
or wisdom,
stupidity
or grace?

6.

Candles go up
in their own smoke.
The apple steeps
in its juices.
Sighing, Eve
steps out of her skin.

The Obligation to Be Happy

It is more onerous
than the rites of beauty
or housework, harder than love.
But you expect it of me casually,
the way you expect the sun
to come up, not in spite of rain
or clouds but because of them.

And so I smile, as if my own fidelity
to sadness were a hidden vice—
that downward tug on my mouth,
my old suspicion that health
and love are brief irrelevancies,
no more than laughter in the warm dark
strangled at dawn.

Happiness. I try to hoist it
on my narrow shoulders again—
a knapsack heavy with gold coins.
I stumble around the house,
bump into things.
Only Midas himself
would understand.

Letter

It is December in the garden,
an early winter here, with snow
already hiding my worst offenses—
the places I disturbed your moss
with my heavy boots; the corner
where I planted in too deep a hole
the now stricken hawthorne: crystals
hanging from its icy branches
are the only flowers it will know.

When did solitude become
mere loneliness and the sounds
of birds at the feeder seem
not like a calibrated music
but the discordant dialects
of strangers simply flying through?
I have tried to construct a life
alone here—coffee at dawn; a jog
through the chilling air

counting my heartbeats,
as if the doctor were my only muse;
books and bread and firewood—
those usual stepping-stones from month
to freezing month. But the constricted light,
the year closing down on itself with all
the vacancies of January ahead, leave me
unreconciled even to beauty.
When will you be coming back?

Snowstorm

Just watching is enough,
as if the eyes were two headlamps,
the body a stalled vehicle
in all this whiteness;
and every space is filled
and filled again with the silence
of pure geometry.
Until, as in a blink, the clouds
part, the fuse

of the sun ignites a passion
of melting, a roar
down the rooftiles,
and here comes the world
as it was, untransformed,
ordinary; and I am still
at the window, full
of a cold knowledge
I hardly understand.

Wind Chill

The door of winter
is frozen shut,

and like the bodies
of long extinct animals, cars

lie abandoned wherever
the cold road has taken them.

How ceremonious snow is,
with what quiet severity

it turns even death to a formal
arrangement.

Alone at my window, I listen
to the wind,

to the small leaves clicking
in their coffins of ice.

Red Fox

The quick red fox trots so casually
across the frozen grass

I think it is a neighbor's dog
until I see that russet tail,

that triangle of face—
more emblem than animal.

There is no slyness
in the way he moves, no whiff

of wild grape or hunter's horn.
But fact and fable intersect

for just as long as it takes him
to lay his tracks down

on our suburban snow
and disappear.

Deer

To the secret places
of the garden, deer come
eating their way through
the milky blossoms of impatiens,
the blur of azalea leaves.
How enigmatic their eyes are
and how swiftly they move.
With their soft mouths
they destroy
everything we grew.

A Craving for Salt

Because I don't trust the future,
I look back over my shoulder
wherever I go, like one of those fish
with eyes at the back of its head, or an owl
who swivels its face around full circle.

And though the past is made up
of ordinary things, they smolder
in the heat of afterlight
until memory becomes longing,
as strong as a craving for salt.

Ask Lot's wife who knew
that what she left behind
was simply everything.

Notes to My Mother

1.

Your letters to me
are forwarded to my dreams
where you appear in snatches
of the past, wearing
appropriate clothes—
a thirties' shirtwaist or the long
seal coat you wintered in.
And since your gravestone
is shaped like the front
of our old mailbox,
I'll try to leave my messages
of flowers there.

2.

"Feeling fine, having a good time."
I had to stamp those words
on postcards home from camp,
though I was so homesick there
I'd read the nametapes on my socks
and handkerchiefs—scraps of my real self
you had sewn on by hand.
And so I write it now, though
I'm still homesick eight years after
you left me in my life for good:
feeling fine, having a good time.

3.

The roles of wife and mother
matched you with yourself

as perfectly as your shoes matched
your handbags. Therefore, for years

I couldn't understand my own failures
at order and optimism.

4.

How many autumns I've tried to pick my life up
like a dropped stitch and just get on with it,
tried to pretend the falling temperatures,
the emptying trees were not a synopsis:
so many losses behind me, so many
still ahead. The world is diminished leaf
by single leaf, person by person
and with excruciating slowness.
Sometimes I wish some wandering
comet would hit, as the newspaper
this morning warns or promises—some stray
pinball ricocheting through space.
Then we'd go up together in a lovely blast
of fireworks like the kind I watched
from our July 4th window light up
the sky with percussive neon ribbons.
And the dog, in his last month, hid
under the couch; and your great-grandchildren
couldn't decide whether to be frightened
or ecstatic, their laughter had that edge
of shrillness to it. They don't know
that danger is the shadow thrown
by every bright object; that even family love
can show this dull metallic underside,

as the leaves do which move in sudden gusts
of September wind all in the same direction,
like a school of panicked minnows
sensing a predator ahead.

5.

Though I learned to love
the woman you became
after the stroke,

I never quite forgave her
for hiding my real mother—you,
somewhere

in the drifted snows beyond
that unscalable
widow's peak.

6.

Everywhere
the stream
of life goes on,
and I try to
go with it,
non-swimmer,
paddler in a leaky
canoe.

7.

You taught me always
to write thank you notes, though
I never thanked you properly,
not even when you were dying. But
I thought our inarticulateness

in the face of love was as elemental
as the silence of stones
in the same streambed. I thought
you wanted it that way.

8.

As I grow older, I try
to draw the world in close
as if it were a shawl you had crocheted for me
from small indulgences—morning coffee
from the same cracked cup,
a stroll downhill past empty mailboxes
where only weather may be different
or the seasonal colors of the birds.
And I try to think of loss as a salt sea
I'll learn to swim in later,
getting closer to you
with every overarm stroke.

9.

Things I refuse to think about
also come back in dreams:
the way my fingers have started
to fail, as yours did, knuckle
by swollen knuckle. Last night
I dreamed of handcuffs,
amputation.
Or how even repented sins
are ours for good: they drift
down the exotic rivers
of medicinal sleep,
mewling like kittens.

So in the last moments of wakefulness
I re-create that lost world

whose textures are like braille
beneath my fingertips: the enamel
of the forties' stove where you taught me
to cook; the floral wallpaper you chose
whose roses had no thorns;
the strictness of starch against skin.
And here sleep comes
with all its complicated gifts
and treacheries to gather me
in its arms.

Self-Portrait

after Adam Zagajewski

I am child to no one, mother to a few,
wife for the long haul.
On fall days I am happy
with my dying brethren, the leaves,
but in spring my head aches
from the flowery scents.
My husband fills a room with Mozart
which I turn off, embracing
the silence as if it were an empty page
waiting for me alone to fill it.
He digs in the black earth
with his bare hands. I scrub it
from the creases of his skin, longing
for the kind of perfection
that happens in books.
My house is my only heaven.
A red dog sleeps at my feet, dreaming
of the manic wings of flushed birds.
As the road shortens ahead of me
I look over my shoulder
to where it curves back
to childhood, its white line
bisecting the real and the imagined
the way the ridgepole of the spine
divides the two parts of the body, leaving
the soft belly in the center
vulnerable to anything.
As for my country, it blunders along
as well intentioned as Eve choosing
cider and windfalls, oblivious
to the famine soon to come.
I stir pots, bury my face in books, or hold
a telephone to my ear as if its cord
were the umbilicus of the world

whose voices still whisper to me
even after they have left
their bodies.

Proclamation at a Birth

for Anna

Let every tree
burst into blossom
whatever the season.
Let the snow melt
mild as milk
and the new rain wash
the gutters clean
of last year's
prophecies.
Let the guns sweep out
their chambers
and the criminals doze
dreaming themselves
back to infancy.
Let the sailors throw
their crisp white caps
as high as they can
which like so many doves
will return to the ark
with lilacs.
Let the frogs turn
into princes,
the princes to frogs.
Let the madrigals,
let the musical croakings
begin.

The Newborn

Even in sleep her face changes,
as if every weather
were passing over its surface
just for a moment: sun
and storms, a chill
at the nostrils, the moderating
climate of a half formed smile.
They are all there, the emotions
that are not yet even a dream
in her future. You can see them
in the way the fist uncurls
at the end of her arm
like a long stemmed rose,
or in the frantic way
her mouth searches, driven now
by a craving for milk,
that old thirst in the genes.

Anna at 18 Months

Just as it did
for Eve,
language comes
tumbling in, word
by parroted word
as the world
is named again—
each beast and plant,
each bird.
For the floodgates
are open wide
and out of her dauntless
mouth spill
rough-hewn syllables
for elbow, eyes,
for chin.
And touched
by the wand
of the word, roused
from the alphabet's sleep,
new thoughts flutter awake
like butterflies utterly
changed,
like her damp flirtatious
lashes, beating
their tiny wings.

This Enchanted Forest

"Now it's time for us to go.
We must get out of this
enchanted forest . . ."

—"HANSEL AND GRETEL"

1. RUMPELSTILTSKIN

He was my darling muse,
coming to me as I sat there
struggling with all those
inert words: conjunctions and
prepositions, buts and ifs
and afters—the whole
long grammar of despair.
I remember the pure exhilaration
of ease, like sunlight
on that first bale of straw
and how we laughed together
to see it. I even forgot
the audience who thought
a realm of gold could be built
like a street of glitzy hotels.
He taught me everything.
And after I cheated him,
I had to learn to live
with silence again, the way
the astronauts must learn
to live in thinner air.
If only he'd come back,
I'd give him anything.

2. SNOW WHITE

During REM sleep, my eyelids
flicker in rough pentameter
as I dream of knives

and spoons cohabiting
in their dim drawer,
of pillowslips filled
with forest flowers—
the perfect domestic
tranquillity of an empty house
and me well out of it.

This deep in the woods,
the snow is as pure
as an empty page.
I want the prince
to keep away, to proclaim
the old queen fairest
in the land. I want
all seven of them
to leave me alone
in my long, glass study.

3. THE PRINCESS AND THE PEA

It isn't the insistent
moon, glazing

the dormer window
that keeps me awake.

It's the small, hard
lump of an extra syllable

prodding me through
all seven mattresses.

4. THE ELVES AND THE SHOEMAKER

They say imagination festers
as you sleep, that only hard labor
matters, the hammering
of tack after gleaming tack.

But temperament counts too,
a mix of kindness with
the usual despair.
So when the smell of coffee

rouses me each morning,
I go down to a row
of pages perfectly
sized and metaphored.

Those small ghost writers
have done the work I know
they couldn't have done
without me.

5. GRETEL

"I'm looking back at my white kitten on the roof. . . ."
"That's not your kitten, that's the morning sun on the chimney . . ."

—"HANSEL AND GRETEL"

I am leaving a trail of poems
behind me as I go, words
a bird may find and devour
or rain may wash away,
but it doesn't matter.
It isn't immortality I'm after,
and it's far too late
to find my way back.
For Hansel is married.
The witch may turn up
anywhere. Even my forest
is disappearing,
trunk by toppling trunk.
But I love the feel
of a pen in my hand
like a good stout
walking stick. I love
the way language can trick you

with words like "father"
and "mother," anointing
even the site of treachery
with syllables
such as "cottage" and "home."
Let these crumbs I scatter
nourish some finch
or robin. Let the rain
that washes my words away
be warm on somebody's face.
I know most endings
are unhappy, and the time
for my own fiery one
is approaching so fast
all I can try to do
is set it to music.

Anon.

for Gil

We mustn't speak the name
of God, we're told,
who made the world
just for the love
of making and chose
to be anonymous.

"The small rain down
can rain . . ." a poet said.
And someone stained the glass
for light to pour through,
washing the set stones
in color.

RSVP Regrets Only

I regret that I can't come.
I regret the moment we met
and the way you pretended.
I regret the sun that day,
its warmth so artificial,
and I regret the way pain
has taught me nothing.
I regret this invitation,
its phony formality, its ink
coming off like sin
on my clean fingers.
Since the day I met you,
I regret everything.

Fall in the Literary Review

Though we're pages apart this time,
just being in the same issue
is like being at a party together,
you in your semi-formal attire,
me with my ragged lines,
somber again, but willing
to share a drink or two,
even to exchange a literary joke.
And because we won't ever meet,

because the only sheets we'll share
are pages in a magazine,
you don't mind how old I am,
and I don't care what you look like
or if you're married,
as your poem this time implies.
I don't even care who the lucky "you" is
you keep addressing. I like
to think it's me.

Still Life

Still Life the artist called
these pears and apricots
placed on a blue tablecloth
next to the leather pouch of hares,
tied by their slender ears
like so many vegetables.

But *nature morte,* the French
would say, articulating "dead"
as if to tell us life is less
than life without a hare in the field,
without the actual taste
of pear on the tongue.

Nature Morte

When the last wild asparagus,
waving its ferny head, had escaped
from the garden; when
the last molting dandelion

and the last beet—that purple
underground sun, had crept
under the garden fence
and entered the world,

it was clear that Eden
was over for good.
Now the innocent vegetables
and flowers, freed

of even their names
for only an instant,
have become emblems
of beauty

and appetite, cut off
at the stem or wrenched
from the earth and destined
for the table.

Woman Holding a Balance
Vermeer, 1664

The picture within
the picture is *The Last
Judgement,* subdued
as wallpaper in the background.
And though the woman
holding the scales
is said to be weighing
not a pearl or a coin
but the heft of a single soul,
this hardly matters.
It is really the mystery
of the ordinary
we're looking at—the way
Vermeer has sanctified
the same light that enters
our own grimed windows
each morning, touching
a cheek, the fold
of a dress, a jewelry box
with perfect justice.

Carnival Evening
Henri Rousseau, oil on canvas

Despite the enormous evening sky
spreading over most of the canvas,
its moon no more
than a tarnished coin, dull and flat,
in a devalued currency;

despite the trees, so dark themselves,
stretching upward like supplicants,
utterly leafless; despite what could be
a face, rinsed of feeling, aimed
in their direction,

the two small figures
at the bottom of this picture glow
bravely in their carnival clothes,
as if the whole darkening world
were dimming its lights for a party.

from

A PERFECT CIRCLE OF SUN,

1971

*

Arcadia

There is always a bare house,
one cumulous tree balanced
at the rim of the second story,
emblematic fields the color of change.
We almost find it beyond
the drawn shade of the bus,
beyond the drawn eyelid where light flickers westward,
at the far end of the train whistle
as we travel with George Willard,
with Nick Carroway, travel
towards Christmas and a house
wrapped as safely in scenery
as the corn in its layers of husk.
Birds fly past the chimney,
grow smaller,
disappear as the house disappears around
the flung arm of the road—
solid as a dream at the moment of waking.

January, 7 A.M.

Albino morning.
Windows like milk glass.
Pale sun, pink-eyed;
paler moon frozen
fast to the flagpole's
tip, like the boy's tongue
in the old winter
story.

      Cold travels
the shallow nerve bed
with intimations
of toothache coming,
coming. Early cars
trail their exhausts thick
as the icy breath
of the milkman's horse,
long ago pastured.

At the Gynecologist's

The body so carefully
contrived for pain,
wakens from the dream of health
again and again
to hands impersonal as wax
and instruments that pry
into the closed chapters of flesh.
See me here, my naked legs
caught in these metal stirrups,
galloping towards death
with flowers of ether in my hair.

Notes from the Delivery Room

Strapped down,
victim in an old comic book,
I have been here before,
this place where pain winces
off the walls
like too bright light.
Bear down a doctor says,
foreman to sweating laborer,
but this work, this forcing
of one life from another
is something that I signed for
at a moment when I would have signed anything.
Babies should grow in fields;
common as beets or turnips
they should be picked and held
root end up, soil spilling
from between their toes—
and how much easier it would be later,
returning them to earth.
Bear up . . . bear down . . . the audience
grows restive, and I'm a new magician
who can't produce the rabbit
from my swollen hat.
She's crowning, someone says,
but there is no one royal here,
just me, quite barefoot,
greeting my barefoot child.

Dirge

"The extent of injury which can be directly attributed
to occupation reached astounding proportions in the U.S . . . ."

—*Industrial Hygiene*, by
WILSON SMILLIE

The poets are falling, falling
like leaves on a wind of their own words:
Dylan Thomas over the sheer edge of America;
Sylvia Plath (witch and Gretel combined)
into the hospitable oven.

The poets are plugging the dike with words,
then walking calmly into the sea.
Hart Crane on a Wednesday in slippery April,
Randall Jarrell, Delmore Schwartz, Weldon Kees.
And at the factory

girls paint time's face with radium
and slowly burn; miners slip, hand over hand,
into the blind grave.
Only poets safe at their desks hear death years away,
and full of the intensity of words,
rush to meet it.

Skylight

I sit in a perfect circle of sun
in a room without windows
where pale walls grow stencilled flowers
and see the tops of real trees,
see real leaves flickering in the light
as the tongues of garter snakes flicker
or flattening under an east wind
as if they grew in rushing water.
I think of a ruined church in Rome
where a boy in a blue shirt threw sticks
at a wall that had disappeared
who knows when,
or of something I only read of,
a man whose stomach was a window
doctors gazed through at organs
opening for food like tropic plants
beneath the floor of a glass-bottomed boat.
and here in the center of this house
deep under shingles, under tar paper,
under plaster pale as unsunnned flesh
I see through one round skylight the real world
held up to the sun by its heels and moving—
it is like candling eggs.

Emily Dickinson

We think of her hidden in a white dress
among the folded linens and sachets
of well-kept cupboards, or just out of sight
sending jellies and notes with no address
to all the wondering Amherst neighbors.
Eccentric as New England weather
the stiff wind of her mind, stinging or gentle,
blew two half-imagined lovers off.
Yet legend won't explain the sheer sanity
of vision, the serious mischief
of language, the economy of pain.

At the Jewish Museum
"The Lower East Side:
Portal to American Life,
1887–1924"

We can endure the eyes
of these children lightly,
because they stare
from the faces of our fathers
who have grown old before us.
Their hungers have always been
our surfeit. We turn again
from the rank streets, from
marred expectancies and laundry
that hangs like a portent
over everything.
Here in a new museum
we walk past all the faces
the cameras have stolen from time.
We carry them like piecework
to finish at home,
knowing how our childrens' sins
still fall upon the old Jew
in a coal cellar, on Ludlow street,
in nineteen hundred.

Passover

1.

I set my table with metaphor:
the curling parsley—green sign nailed to the doors
of God's underground; salt of desert and eyes;
the roasted shank bone of a Paschal Lamb,
relic of sacrifice and bleating spring.
Down the long table, past fresh shoots of a root
they have been hacking at for centuries,
you hold up the unleavened bread—a baked scroll
whose wavy lines are undecipherable.

2.

The wise son and the wicked, the simple son
and the son who doesn't ask, are all my son
leaning tonight as it is written,
slouching his father calls it. His hair is long:
hippie hair, hassid hair, how strangely alike
they seem tonight. First Born, a live child cried
among the bulrushes, but the only root
you know stirs between your legs, ready
to spill its seed in gentile gardens.
And if the flowers be delicate and fair,
I only mind this one night of the year
when far beyond the lights of Jersey,
Jerusalem still beckons us, in tongues.

3.

What black-throated bird
in a warm country
sings spirituals,
sings spirituals
to Moses now?

4.

One exodus prefigures the next.
The glaciers fled before hot whips of air.
Waves bowed at God's gesture
for fugitive Israel to pass;
while fish, caught then behind windows
of water, remembered how their brothers once
pulled themselves painfully from the sea,
willing legs to grow
from slanted fins.
Now the blossoms pass from April's tree,
refugee raindrops mar the glass,
borders are transitory.
And the changeling gene, still seeking
stone sanctuary, moves on.

5.

Far from Egypt, I have sighted blood,
have heard the throaty mating of frogs.
My city knows vermin, animals loose in hallways,
boils, sickness, hail.
In the suburban gardens
seventeen-year locusts rise
from their heavy beds
in small explosions of sod.
Darkness of newsprint.
My son, my son.

The Last Train

"The long-distance passenger train has moved one step nearer to
extinction: on July 26 The New York Central said it intends to
discontinue all trains running over 200 miles. . . ."

—U.S. News and World Report

There may have been a boy,
lying in a cabin in the subtle place
where field and plain each goes its separate way,
who fell asleep to the muffled drumming of buffalo
as, dark and shaggy as sleep itself,
they traveled past his window towards extinction.

Now in a house at the edge of the same plain,
another boy lets consciousness recede
on the receding whistle of a train
passing his open window for the last time,
leaving behind a spike or rusted nails
like arrowheads or pieces of dried bone.

So we are left,
each boy, each sleeper,
to the single, abstract tone of the jet plane.
We follow sleep as well as we are able
along disintegrating paths of vapor,
high above the dreamlike shapes of clouds.

To a Second Son

Now you embrace chameleons
changing color yourself with the scenery,
white with me and my white questions,
muted under a sky bruised
black and blue.

You feed your lizards
moths, plundered each evening
from the porch light
while my shudder records
as accurately as a seismograph
the distance between us.

Peter, we have given you
these hand-me-downs:
your brother's half-used sweater,
your father's reel,
and all my old faults
drowned once like a bagful of cats.

They have washed up twenty years downstream
bloated and mewing, to plague
the perfect body you will grow into,
shaking all of us delicately off.

Beech Avenue: The Fourth of July

How heavy the summer seems, how thick-waisted
and full of heat. The elm is swollen with leaves,
and the lowing clouds, still filled with rain,
hang pendulous as unmilked udders.
The air tastes faintly of cordite where
a Roman candle flickers and is snuffed out.
One by one the minutes gather and spill
over the rim of my cupped hands, and I
watch as though already remembering
these friends scattered like spit watermelon seeds
over the garden; Rachel holding
her first amazing sparkler; the boys
running through grass away from us, from
the whole green day which nonetheless will keep
hard as a pebble around which moss will grow
and lichen. Where shall I be on that July
when the pebble cracks like a geode,
and there perfectly preserved in layers
of crystal my grown sons find these very
trees, short-circuited with fireflies,
this restless lightning, locked in cloud but
hammering out now, sparks flying, as rain
hesitant all day finally starts to fall?

There Is a Figure in Every Landcape

There is a figure in every landscape—
a boy at the other end of the pier,
a woman picking dandelions for salad
who leaves a kneeprint hidden in the grass
like the watermark on whitest paper.
That crooked branch is really a girl's arm
sunned to the very color of the bark,
an oval leaf conceals an oval eye:
children are climbing here, or have been.
Even in Adam's garden in the green
newness of unused shade, distrusting
privacy, God placed a sleeping woman.

Libation, 1966

We used to sacrifice young girls,
killing them like does
on rocky altars
they themselves had kept
tidy as kitchens.

Moloch took babies,
picked them early
from their mother's limbs
like green fruit,
spat out the pits.

It always was for some necessity,
fat harvest,
rain,
wind for a flaccid ocean, sails
flapping like gulls' wings towards Troy.

Now we give young men.
They dance as delicately
as any bull boy,
with bayonet,
in a green maze,
under a sky as hot as Crete.

Between Generations

I left my father in a wicker basket
on other people's doorsteps.
Now I wait to be adopted by children,
wait in a house far between generations
with night rising faster
than the moon.

I dream of Regan laughing on her father's lap
behind the castle.
I laughed once in my father's face,
and he laughed, and the two laughters
locked like bumpers
that still rust away between us.

My children fill the house with departures.
Zippers close, trunks close, wire hangers jump
on the empty pole—ghosts without their sheets.
And I ask what strict gravity
pushes love down the steep incline
from father to child, always down?

October Funeral

for Ag

The world is shedding
its thousand skins.
The snake goes naked,
and the needles of the pine fall out
like the teeth of a comb I broke
upon your hair last week.
The ghosts of dead leaves
haunt no one. Impossible
to give you to the weather,
to leave you locked in a killed tree.
No metaphysic has prepared us
for the simple act of turning
and walking away.

Journey's End

How hard we try to reach death safely,
luggage intact, each child accounted for,
the wounds of passage quickly bandaged up.
We treat the years like stops along the way
of a long flight from the catastrophe
we move to, thinking: home free all at last.
Wave, wave your hanky towards journey's end;
avert your eyes from windows grimed with twilight
where landscapes rush by, terrible and lovely.

A Dangerous Time

November is a dangerous time for trees;
November is a dangerous time.
The leaves darken,
the sun goes on and off
beyond strange clouds,
a wolf is at the door.
Upstairs the children toss through dreams,
hearing the wind in the keyholes of sleep,
hearing the sirens circle the house like coyotes.
I have tucked them in with the wolf's own story,
how it grew from a cub, devoured the bride,
blew down the house of straw—
how this was natural.
Now my eldest walks the freezing hills
crying wolf, wolf.
He is a prophet, he has warned before
that the stars will rise like gooseflesh,
and a wolf is at the door.

from

ASPECTS OF EVE,

1975

◆

Rachel

(Rachel [ra'chal], a ewe)

We named you
for the sake
of the syllables
and for the small boat
that followed the *Pequod*,
gathering lost children
of the sea.

We named you
for the dark-eyed girl
who waited by the well
while her lover
worked seven years
and again
seven.

We named you
for the small daughters
of the Holocaust
who followed their six-pointed stars
to death
and were all of them
known as
Rachel.

Night Sounds

When the clock
like a moon shows
the dark side of its face
we reach
across cold expanses
of pillow
for speech.
In that silence
a fox barks
from the next field,
or a train drags its long syllable
over a hill,
or the baby
washed up again from sleep
sends its vowels
calling
for their lost
consonants.

A Real Story

Sucking on hard candy
to sweeten the taste
of old age,
grandpa told us stories
about chickens,
city chickens sold
for Sabbath soup
but rescued at the end
by some chicken-loving
providence.

Now at ninety-five,
sucked down
to nothing himself,
he says he feels
a coldness;
perhaps the coldness David felt
even with Abishag
in his bed
to warm
his chicken-thin bones.

But when we say
you'll soon get well,
grandpa pulls the sheet
over his face,
raising it between us
the way he used to raise
the Yiddish paper
when we said
enough chickens
tell us a real story.

Go Gentle

You have grown wings of pain
and flap around the bed like a wounded gull
calling for water, calling for tea, for grapes
whose skins you cannot penetrate.
Remember when you taught me
how to swim? Let go, you said,
the lake will hold you up.
I long to say, Father let go
and death will hold you up.
Outside the fall goes on without us.
How easily the leaves give in,
I hear them on the last breath of wind,
passing this disappearing place.

Wildflowers

You gave me dandelions.
They took our lawn
by squatters' rights—
round suns rising
in April, soft moons
blowing away in June.
You gave me lady slippers,
bloodroot, milkweed,
trillium whose secret number
the children you gave me
tell. In the hierarchy
of flowers, the wild
rise on their stems
for naming.
Call them weeds.
I pick them as I
picked you,
for their fierce,
unruly joy.

Folk Tale

All knobs and knuckles, hammer knees and elbows
they were a multitude of two, man and woman
dwelling as one tight flesh. In hallways,
on stairs vaguely lit by twilight, in their own
meager bed they would collide . . . veer off . . .
collide, like aging children aiming those
bumper cars, madly in Kansas Coney Islands.
Blue sparks jumped on their ceiling, lit her stockings
strangling his faucet, his fist plumbing
her shoulder's depth for blood. Until, as it is told,
they brought the cow into the house, straight from the barn,
oppressed for years with milk. They tied it,
lowing, to the icebox, pastured it
on rubber plants and dusty philodendrons.
They brought the horse in next, leaving the plow
like an abandoned aircraft, nose down
in rusting fields of corn. The pig, the donkey,
the rooster with its crowd of hens, they even
brought a neighbor's child complete with spelling words
and scales that wandered up and down the untuned
piano searching for roost as the chickens
searched and the cow, nuzzling the humming
frigidaire as if it were a calf.

2.

So they survived with all that cuckoo's brood,
hearing the horse stamp through the floorboards,
the donkey chew the welcome mat, and all night long
through tumbling barricades of sleep the yeasty
rise and fall of breath. By blue television light
they milked and gathered, boiled the placid eggs
that turned up everywhere, laughed with the child,
fed the pig, and glimpsed each other's rounded limbs

reflected for a moment in the copper
washtub or around the feathers of a settling hen.
And winter passed; and spring; and summer.
The child left first, all braided, for the school bus.
The cow died of old griefs. The horse dreaming
of harness, the pig of swill, the donkey
of what magnitude of straw, broke out one night
and emptied the ark. Man and woman leaning
on brooms stood at the kitchen door and waved,
saw through a blaze of autumn the cock's comb
like one last, bright leaf flutter and disappear.
Then jostling a bit, for ceremony's sake,
they turned and lost themselves in so much space.

Death's Blue-Eyed Girl

When did the garden with its banked flowers
start to smell like a funeral chapel,
and the mild breeze passing our foreheads
to feel like the back of a nurse's hand
testing for fever? We used to be
immortal in our ignorance, sending
our kites up for the lightning, swimming
in unknown waters at night and naked.
Death was a kind of safety net to catch us
if we fell too far. Remember Elaine
standing in April, a child on one hip
for ballast, her head distracted with poems?
The magician waved and bowed, showed us his
empty sleeves and she was gone.

To Consider a House

"Eden is that old-fashioned House
we dwell in every day . . ."

—EMILY DICKINSON

When Eden closed like a fist
around a penny,
like a flower whose petals contract
at the first touch
of weather,
when only fire was left to warn,
as fire warns the wild animals;
and even before Cain
had come to start
what we have never ended;
it was time then, for the first time,
to consider a house.
Before, they had rested
carelessly, naming a tree
then sleeping under it,
or sleeping first
and naming later. Now,
the soul shaken loose
from the body,
in temporary residence only
in their skin,
they dreamed the safety
of boxes within boxes,
of doors closing quietly
on doors.
They traveled East,
not following the sun
but drawn, as if by accident, back
to its source.
The animals too had fled, taking
only their names with them.

So as the birds learned,
they learned
to build of scraps,
of sticks and straws collected
along the way.
With the beaver they saw
what can be dammed up,
how to make use of all
that accumulates.
And like the bear they took
the hollowness of caves,
a shape to be confirmed
by the still untested womb.
In their own image they built their house:
eyelike windows, blank
with light; a skeleton of beams;
clay walls, crumbling a little,
as flesh was already learning
to crumble.
And from the hearth,
the smoldering center of the house, smoke
rose up the chimney
each morning, each dusk
making the leap toward God
that always ended
in cloud.
Only much later,
and hesitantly at first,
they thought to plant
another garden.

You Are Odysseus

You are Odysseus
returning home each evening
tentative, a little angry.
And I who thought to be
one of the Sirens (cast up
on strewn sheets
at dawn)
hide my song
under my tongue—
merely Penelope after all.
Meanwhile the old wars
go on, their dim music
can be heard even at night.
You leave each morning,
soon our son will follow.
Only my weaving is real.

Butter

You held the butter-
cup under my chin
and laughed: "get thee
to a buttery,"
chewing on a dandelion stem,
then tasting my
buttery fingers
one by one
and eying
my breasts as if
they too could,
bobbing, churn
pure milk to
butter.
Yellow dress and
flowers, yellow
hair, the world
was melting butter
sweet and slick,
your hands all yellow
with the spilling
sun, desire
like the heated
knife through
butter.

Knots

In the retreating tide
of light,
among bulrushes
and eelgrass
my small son teaches
my stuttering hands
the language of sailor's knots.

I tell him how
each Jewish bride
was given a knotted chaos
of yarn
and told to order it
into a perfect sphere,
to prove she'd be a patient wife.

Patient, impatient son
I've unknotted shoestrings,
kitestrings, tangled hair.
But standing at high windows
enclosed in the domestic rustle
of birds and leaves
I've dreamed of knotting
bedsheets together
to flee by.

Block

I place one word slowly
in front of the other,
like learning to walk again
after an illness.
But the blank page
with its hospital corners
tempts me.
I want to lie down
in its whiteness
and let myself drift
all the way back
to silence.

Drift

Lying in bed this morning
you read to me of continental drift,
how Africa and South America
sleeping once side by side
slowly slid apart;
how California even now
pushes off like a swimmer
from the country's edge, along
the San Andreas fault.
And I thought about you and me
who move in sleep each night
to the far reaches of the bed,
ranges of blanket between us.
It is a natural law this drift
and though we break it
as we break bread
over and over again, you remain
Africa with your deep shade,
your heat. And I, like California,
push off from your side
my two feet cold
against your back, dreaming
of Asia Minor.

Popcorn

When Plato said
that what we see are shadows
flickering on a cave wall,
he must have meant
the movies.
You let a cigarette lean
from your mouth precisely
as Bogart did.
Because of this, reels later,
we say of our life
that it is B-grade;
that it opened and will close
in a dusty place where
things move always
in slow motion;
that what is real
is the popcorn
jammed between our teeth.

Sacred to Apollo

Sometimes I am Daphne.
My sleeves rustle in the wind,
and I feel the green root
of the bay, nourishing
or aching with the season.

And I have been Niobe,
all mother, all tears,
but myself somewhere hidden
in the essential stone.

You say I write
like a man
and expect me
to smile.

Or you hold me as though
I would break; and indeed
I come apart in your hands
like pieces of a vast
and unsolved puzzle.

Perhaps it is Apollo
I still flee from
despite his music
and his healing ways.

Now I paint my mouth
red for blood,
and in its twistings,
secret as any river,
I am Helen again
and dangerous.

Aspects of Eve

To have been one
of many ribs
and to be chosen.
To grow into something
quite different
knocking finally
as a bone knocks
on the closed gates of the garden—
which unexpectedly
open.

After Agatha Christie

in the locked room
what cannot happen
happens again
shaped to the size
of a keyhole
death comes reassuring
choosing someone
no one will miss
now everything becomes
a clue
the moon has left
footprints
all over the rug
the tree outside
the window
hides behind
its false beard
of leaves
who did what
precisely when
slyly the clock stops
the blood smells of ink
the revolver shows
its pearl handle
at the end the facts
click into place
comfortably as knitting
each answer marries
its proper question
even the skull
smiles to itself
as the detective tells
how the moon was pure
all along
the tree was merely

a tree
and only I
have no alibi
at all

Algebra

I used to solve equations easily.
If train A left Sioux Falls
at nine o'clock, traveling
at a fixed rate,
I knew when it would meet train B.
Now I wonder if the trains will crash;
or else I picture naked limbs
through Pullman windows, each
a small vignette of longing.

And I knew X, or thought I did,
shuttled it back and forth
like a poor goat
across the equals sign.
X was the unknown on a motor bike,
those autumn days when leaves flew past
the color of pencil shavings.
Obedient as a genie, it gave me answers
to what I thought were questions.

Unsolved equations later, and winter now,
I know X better than I did.
His is the scarecrow's bitter mouth
sewn shut in cross-stitch;
the footprint of a weasel on snow.
X is the unknown assailant.
X marks the spot
toward which we speed like trains,
at a fixed rate.

Eclipse

A few minutes past noon:
the birds begin their evening songs
and break for the trees;
the horse nods in its dimming stall.
Afraid of a truth that could blind
I turn my cold shoulder to the sun
and catch its shadow in a cardboard box
as though it were some rare bug
about to be effaced by the moon's
slow thumb. To catalog is not enough.
What did Adam know, naming the apple?
What do the astronomers suspect?
The sun like a swallowed sword
comes blazing back.
It is not chaos
I fear in this strange dusk
but the inexplicable order of things.

A Symposium: Apples

Eve   Remember a season
of apples, the orchard
full of them, my apron
full of them? One day
we wandered from tree
to tree, sharing a basket
feeling the weight of apples
increase between us.
And how your muscles ripened
with all that lifting.
I felt them round and hard
under my teeth; white
and sweet the flesh
of men and apples.

Gabriel   Nameless in Eden,
the apple itself
was innocent—an ordinary
lunchpail fruit.
Still it reddened
for the way it was used.
Afterward the apple
chose for itself
names untrusting
on the tongue: stayman,
gravenstein,
northern spy.

The   Ordinary, innocent
Serpent yes. But deep
in each center of whiteness
one dark star . . .

Adam   In the icebox
an apple
will keep
for weeks.
Then its skin
wrinkles up
like the skin of the old man
I have become,
from a single
bite.

from
THE FIVE STAGES
OF GRIEF,
1978

◆

Funerary Tower: Han Dynasty

"The meaning of the figures carrying babies
in their arms is not clear."

In this season of salt
leaves drop away
revealing the structure
of the trees.

Good bones,
as my father would say
drawing the hair from my face.
I'd pull impatiently away.

Today we visit my father's grave.
My mother housekeeps, with trowel
among the stones,
already at home here.

Impatient, even at forty
I hurry her home.
We carry our childhoods
in our arms.

After

After the month
in Sicily,
the ocean's edge unravelling
around our own
volcanic knees;
after the dark plums
that throbbed like fairy-tale hearts
in the woodsman's basket;
the voyage in another's arms
where we were innocent
as tourists
visiting familiar landscapes
for the first time

we come back
to our old lives
as to a heap of clothes
we have left in our closet,
and either they have shrunk
or we have grown fat
on the risen cream
of ease.
But soon our old possessions
cry out
like artifacts
not to be buried yet.
We are claimed

by our dishes, by their need
to be washed and dried
and put away;
by our mattress which like a pliant wife
has shaped itself
to our remembered bodies.
And at the edge of the grass

our deaths wait like domestic animals.
They have been there all along,
patient and loving.
We must hurry
or we may miss them
in the swelling dark.

Egg

In this kingdom
the sun never sets;
under the pale oval
of the sky
there seems no way in
or out,
and though there is a sea here
there is no tide.

For the egg itself
is a moon
glowing faintly
in the galaxy of the barn,
safe but for the spoon's
ominous thunder,
the first delicate crack
of lightning.

Voices

Joan heard voices
and she burned for it.
Driving through the dark
I write poems.
Last night I drove through
a stop sign, pondering
line breaks.
When I explained
the policeman nodded,
then he gave me
a ticket.
Someone who knows told me
writers have fifteen years,
then comes repetition,
even madness.
Like Midas, I guess
everything we touch turns
to a poem—
when the spell is on.
But think of the poet after that
touching the trees
he's always touched,
but this time nothing happens.
Picture him rushing from trunk
to trunk, bruising
his hands on the rough bark.
Only five years left.
Sometimes I bury
my poems in the garden,
saving them
for the cold days ahead.
One way or another
you burn for it.

In the Old Guerilla War

In the old guerilla war
between father and son
I am the no-man's-land.
When the moon shows
over my scorched breast
they fire across me.
If a bullet ricochets
and I bleed, they say
it is my time of month.
Sometimes I iron
handkerchiefs
into flags of truce,
hide them in pockets;
or humming, I roll socks
instead of bandages.
Then we sit down together
breaking only bread.
The family tree
shades us, the snipers
waiting in its branches
sleep between green leaves.
I think of the elm
sending its roots
like spies underground
through any rough terrain
in search of water; or Noah
sending out the dove
to find land.
Only survive long enough;
the triggers will rust into rings
around both their fingers.
I will be a field
where all the flowers
on my housedress
bloom at once.

Marks

My husband gives me an A
for last night's supper,
an incomplete for my ironing,
a B plus in bed.
My son says I am average,
an average mother, but if
I put my mind to it
I could improve.
My daughter believes
in Pass/Fail and tells me
I pass. Wait 'til they learn
I'm dropping out.

It Is Raining on the House of Anne Frank

It is raining on the house
of Anne Frank
and on the tourists
herded together under the shadow
of their umbrellas,
on the perfectly silent
tourists who would rather be
somewhere else
but who wait here on stairs
so steep they must rise
to some occasion
high in the empty loft,
in the quaint toilet,
in the skeleton
of a kitchen
or on the map—
each of its arrows
a barb of wire—
with all the dates, the expulsions,
the forbidding shapes
of continents.
And across Amsterdam it is raining
on the Van Gogh Museum
where we will hurry next
to see how someone else
could find the pure
center of light
within the dark circle
of his demons.

A Short History of Judaic Thought
in the Twentieth Century

The rabbis wrote:
although it is forbidden
to touch a dying person,
nevertheless, if the house
catches fire
he must be removed
from the house.

Barbaric!
I say,
and whom may I touch then,
aren't we all
dying?

You smile
your old negotiator's smile
and ask:
but aren't all our houses
burning?

Ice Age

The pterodactyl on the roof
spreads its ghostly wings
to shelter us.
In the thermometers
the mercury slides to the bottom
making pools of silver—
we skate on them.
The world's weather is growing cold.
Already glaciers are moving
towards Maryland
where just now a light snow
started to fall,
and women are already knitting mufflers
which will not be thick enough
to warm our throats.
The snow is vague at the windows,
an early symptom.
Later the flakes will multiply,
the house will be wrapped
in a winding sheet of snow
snow like snuff in the nostrils,
like ash in the chimneys.
The children will build a house of snow
and disappear inside it.
Now wooly bears grow thick, black
mourning bands, carrots burrow deep.
I have heard of miller moths
breaking into houses,
have seen my own breath ice mirrors—
they will need no other covering.
We must learn the cold lessons
the dinosaurs learned:
to freeze magnified
in someone else's history;
to leave our bones behind.

Fresco

In Masaccio's *Expulsion*
from the Garden
how benign the angel seems,
like a good civil servant
he is merely enforcing
the rules. I remember
these faces from Fine Arts 13.
I was young enough then
to think that the loss of innocence
was just about Sex.
Now I see Eve covering
her breasts with her hands
and I know it is not to hide them
but only to keep them
from all she must know
is to follow
from Abel on one,
Cain on the other.

Bicentennial Winter

The only revolution is among the oaks
here in the woods;
their mutinous leaves
refuse to fall, despite
the laws of season
and of gravity.
Red-coated cardinals hide
among those leaves.
Red bird, cold weather
the farmers say.
Know us by our myths.
I think of the mutinous
Puritans who taught us
that all things break.
We have forgotten that,
disenchanted;
amazed as children told
for the first time
how they were conceived.
Still the mind moves
continually west, following
paths beaten by the sun
risking ambush
and early darkness.
On Sundays, driving
past frontiers
lit by milkweed
let us find what wilderness
is left. Deep in the woods
it's possible to see the cruelties
between fox and rabbit
and their mutual beauty;
to study the creeks:
how the citizenry of small stones
is washed in waters that run

to the Potomac,
still clear in places,
in places muddy.
Today the river's a frozen slate,
a tabula rasa. It tempts us
as it did two hundred winters ago
to dare the dangerous
freedom of the skater.

Old Woman

In the evening
my griefs come to me
one by one.
They tell me what I had hoped to forget.
They perch on my shoulders
like mourning doves.
They are the color
of light fading.

In the day
they come back
wearing disguises.
I rock and rock
in the warm amnesia of sun.
When my griefs sing to me
from the bright throats of thrushes
I sing back.

Caroline

She wore
her coming death
as gracefully
as if it were a coat
she'd learned to sew.
When it grew cold enough
she'd simply button it
and go.

Consolations

Listen:
language does the best it can.
I speak

the dog whines
and in the changeling trees
late bees mumble, vague

as voices
barely heard
from the next room.

Later
the consolations
of silence.

The nights pass slowly.
I turn their heavy pages
one by one

licking my index finger
as my grandfather did
wanting to close the book on pain.

Afternoons smell of burning.
Already leaves have loosened
on the branch

small scrolls bearing
the old messages
each year.

You touch me—
another language. Our griefs
are almost one;

we swing them between us
like the child lent us awhile
who holds one hand of yours

and one of mine
hurrying us home
as streetlights

start to flower
down the dark stem
of evening.

Geneticist

"I thought you were your father,"
someone said,
seeing for the first time
the blaze of curls around your neck
passed down by primogeniture,
though learned
from your own sons.
You spoke of how you used to hide
in a dim sanctuary
of women's shoes
against that father's drunken rage.
You sipped your scotch.

Now you learn the alphabet
of genes, study their silences,
the intricate switch
that turns them on and off
like lightbulbs on a hotel telephone
signalling: someone has left a message.
And the message itself intact
for generations—a letter
that has waited
in some dusty cubbyhole
delivered at last.
Open it!

Because

Because the night you asked me,
the small scar of the quarter moon
had healed—the moon was whole again;
because life seemed so short;
because life stretched before me
like the darkened halls of nightmare;
because I knew exactly what I wanted;
because I knew exactly nothing;
because I shed my childhood with my clothes—
they both had years of wear left in them;
because your eyes were darker than my father's;
because my father said I could do better;
because I wanted badly to say no;
because Stanley Kowalski shouted "Stella . . .";
because you were a door I could slam shut;
because endings are written before beginnings;
because I knew that after twenty years
you'd bring the plants inside for winter
and make a jungle we'd sleep in naked;
because I had free will;
because everything is ordained;
I said yes.

threads to be woven later

my grandmother's grave
like a loaf
of newly risen bread

my father's photograph
dying
in its frame

my mother
whose perfect beauty
I finally forgive

shades at the window
constellations
of dust

the tree of veins
a leaf
of my own blood

loving, being loved
the panicking
of the pulse

the weight
of the baby's head
fragile as a moon

a story
in my son's writing
the mother is the villain

the year
I took to my typewriter
as others take to their bed

words
leaking their meanings
ruining the page

the smell of the sea rising
the rising
of bread

postcard from cape cod

just now I saw
one yellow
butterfly
migrating
across buzzard's bay
how brave I thought
or foolish
like sending
a poem
across months
of silence
and on such
delicate
wings

25th High School Reunion

We come to hear the endings
of all the stories
in our anthology
of false starts:
how the girl who seemed
as hard as nails
was hammered
into shape;
how the athletes ran
out of races;
how under the skin
our skulls rise
to the surface
like rocks in the bed
of a drying stream.
Look! We have all
turned into
ourselves.

Arithmetic Lesson: Infinity

"In nature's infinite book of secrecy
a little I can read . . ."
—WILLIAM SHAKESPEARE,
Antony and Cleopatra, I.ii.9

Picture a parade of numbers: 1
the sentry, out in front;
dependent, monogamous 2;
3 that odd man out, that 1 too many
always trying to break into line.
Numbers are subtracted, added
numbers fall by the way.
Some are broken into fractions—torn apart;
some assigned to stars, to crystals
of salt; to threads of water
on the ocean's dragging hem.
The proper numbers march together
their uniform buttons bright;
the rational numbers walk alone.
Every number on every clock repeats
its psalm over again
as minutes are numbered;
and children; and parcels of earth;
each sparrow as it falls;
each leaf after falling, before burning.
The negative numbers squabble
among themselves; imaginary numbers
count the number of kisses
that dance on the head of a pin.
And the parade goes on.
Each leaf of grass is numbered
just as it bends beneath
a numbered foot; each newt;
each spider's egg;
each grain of sleep caught
in each waking eye.

Pages are numbered as they turn;
dreams as they turn
into facts; the sun
as it rises on its fiery stalk
and as it sets.
But just as the end trembles into sight
the way the sea trembles
beyond the final dune
the steps of the marchers
grow smaller and smaller again—
the steps divide. Each number
hangs back, reluctant as a child
afraid of what he'll find
at the end of a darkened hall.
And though the destination
remains at hand
the parade moves slowly on: 1
the sentry, out in front;
dependent, monogamous 2;
3

The Five Stages of Grief

The night I lost you
someone pointed me towards
the Five Stages of Grief.
Go that way, they said,
it's easy, like learning to climb
stairs after the amputation.
And so I climbed.
Denial was first.
I sat down at breakfast
carefully setting the table
for two. I passed you the toast—
you sat there. I passed
you the paper—you hid
behind it.
Anger seemed more familiar.
I burned the toast, snatched
the paper and read the headlines myself.
But they mentioned your departure,
and so I moved on to
Bargaining. What could I exchange
for you? The silence
after storms? My typing fingers?
Before I could decide, *Depression*
came puffing up, a poor relation
its suitcase tied together
with string. In the suitcase
were bandages for the eyes
and bottles of sleep. I slid
all the way down the stairs
feeling nothing.
And all the time Hope
flashed on and off
in defective neon.
Hope was my uncle's middle name,
he died of it.

After a year I am still climbing,
though my feet slip
on your stone face.
The treeline
has long since disappeared;
green is a color
I have forgotten.
But now I see what I am climbing
towards; *Acceptance,*
written in capital letters,
a special headline:
Acceptance,
its name is in lights.
I struggle on,
waving and shouting.
Below, my whole life spreads its surf,
all the landscapes I've ever known
or dreamed of. Below
a fish jumps: the pulse
in your neck.
Acceptance. I finally
reach it.
But something is wrong.
Grief is a circular staircase.
I have lost you.

from

WAITING FOR MY LIFE,

1981

◆

Epilogue

Years later the girl died
no longer a girl,
and the old man fishing
in sullied waters
saw his one mistake
flash by—
but only for a moment.
The moon continued
its periodic rise and fall,
sometimes the shape
of a snow elk's horn,
sometimes a vague
repository of light.
Katerina married
someone else.
Robert, though only a minor character
grew into the hero
of another story.
And the house was rebuilt
by strangers.
Only the lake stayed the same,
its surface equivocal
as the pages of a book
on which everything remains
to be written.

Prologue

Nothing has happened yet.
The house settles
into its stones,
unoccupied;
the road curves
towards something—
away from something else.
A single elk bends
to the lake to drink,
or in the confusion of dusk
perhaps it is simply
an old tree
leaning over the water.
If there were voices,
their language would be
expectancy; but the silence
is nearly perfect.
Even the sun is motionless
before it takes that definite plunge
into the darkness
of the first chapter.

Dreams

Dreams are the only
afterlife we know;
the place where the children
we were
rock in the arms of the children
we have become.

They are as many as leaves
in their migrations,
as birds whose deaths we learn of
by the single feather
left behind: a clue,
a particle of sleep

caught in the eye.
They are as irretrievable as sand
when the sea creeps up
its long knife glittering
in its teeth
to claim its patrimony.

Sometimes my father
in knickers and cap
waits on that shore,
the dream of him
a wound
not even morning can heal.

The dog's legs pump
in his sleep;
your closed eyelids flicker
as the reel unwinds:
watcher and watched,
archer and bull's-eye.

Last night I dreamed a lover in my arms
and woke innocent.
The sky was starry to the very rind,
his smile still burning there
like the tail of a comet
that has just blazed by.

McGuffey's First Eclectic Reader

The sun is up.
The sun is always up.
The silent "e"
keeps watch.
And 26 strong stones
can build a wall of syllables
for Nell and Ned
and Ann.

Rab was such a good dog,
Mother. We left him
under the big tree
by the brook
to take care of the dolls
and the basket.

But Rab has run away.
The basket's gone back to reeds
through which the night wind
blows; and mother was erased;
the dolls are painted harlots
in the Doll's Museum.

Where did it go, Rose?
I don't know;
away off, somewhere.

The fat hen
has left the nest.

I hand my daughter
this dusty book.
Framed in her window
the sky darkens to slate:
a lexicon of wandering stars.

Listen, child—the barking
in the distance
is Rab the Dog Star
trotting home
for dinner.

Secrets

The secrets I keep
from myself
are the same secrets
the leaves keep
from the old trunk of the tree
even as they turn
color.

They are the garbled
secrets
of the waterfall
about to be stunned
on rock;
the sounds of the stream's
dry mouth
after weeks of drought.

Hush, says the nurse
to the new child howling
its one secret
into the world,
hush
as she buries
its mouth
in milk.

On the hearth the fire consumes
its own burning tongue,
I cannot read the ash.
By the gate
the trumpet flower sings
only silence
from its shapely
throat.

At night
I fall asleep
to the whippoorwill's
raucous lullabye,
old as the first garden:
never tell
never tell
never tell.

Waiting for My Life

I waited for my life to start
for years, standing at bus stops
looking into the curved distance
thinking each bus was the wrong bus;
or lost in books where I would travel
without luggage from one page
to another; where the only breeze
was the rustle of pages turning,
and lives rose and set
in the violent colors of suns.

Sometimes my life coughed and coughed:
a stalled car about to catch,
and I would hold someone in my arms,
though it was always someone else I wanted.
Or I would board any bus, jostled
by thighs and elbows that knew
where they were going; collecting scraps
of talk, setting them down like birdsong
in my notebook, where someday I would go
prospecting for my life.

In Back Of

"I'm looking for things back of remarks that are said . . ."

—WILLIAM STAFFORD

In back of "I love you"
stands "goodbye."
In back of
"goodbye"
stands "it was lovely
there in the grass, drenched
in so much green
together."
Words that wait
are dark as shadows
in the back rooms
of mirrors:
when you raise
your right hand
in greeting,
they raise their left
in farewell.

Eyes Only

Dear lost sharer
of silences,
I would send a letter
the way the tree sends messages
in leaves,
or the sky in exclamations
of pure cloud.

Therefore I write
in this blue
ink, color
of secret veins
and arteries.
It is morning here.
Already the postman walks

the innocent streets,
dangerous as Aeolus
with his bag of winds,
or Hermes, the messenger,
god of sleep and dreams
who traces my image
upon this stamp.

In public buildings
letters are weighed
and sorted like meat;
in railway stations
huge sacks of mail
are hidden like robbers' booty
behind freight-car doors.

And in another city
the conjurer
will hold a fan of letters

before your outstretched hand—
"Pick any card . . ."
You must tear the envelope
as you would tear bread.

Only then dark rivers
of ink will thaw
and flow
under all the bridges
we have failed
to build
between us.

Excursion

I am a tourist
in my own life,
gazing at the exotic shapes
of flowers
as if someone else
had planted them;
barred
from the half-lit rooms
of children
by an invisible
velvet rope.
The dresses in my closet
are costumes
for a different woman,
though I hide myself
in their silky textures.
The man asleep
in my bed
knows me best
in the dark.

Meditation by the Stove

I have banked the fires
of my body
into a small but steady blaze,
here in the kitchen
where the dough has a life of its own,
breathing under its damp cloth
like a sleeping child;
where the real child plays under the table,
pretending the tablecloth is a tent,
practicing departures; where a dim
brown bird dazzled by light
has flown into the windowpane
and lies stunned on the pavement—
it was never simple, even for birds,
this business of nests.
The innocent eye sees nothing, Auden says,
repeating what the snake told Eve,
what Eve told Adam, tired of gardens,
wanting the fully lived life.
But passion happens like an accident.
I could let the dough spill over the rim
of the bowl, neglecting to punch it down,
neglecting the child who waits under the table,
the mild tears already smudging her eyes.
We grow in such haphazard ways.
Today I feel wiser than the bird.
I know the window shuts me in,
that when I open it
the garden smells will make me restless.
And I have banked the fires of my body
into a small domestic flame for others
to warm their hands on for a while.

Who Is It Accuses Us?

Who is it accuses us of safety,
as if the family were soldiers
instead of hostages,
as if the garden were not mined
with explosive peonies,
as if the most common death
were not by household accident?
We have chosen the dangerous life.
Consider the pale necks of the children
under their colored head scarves,
the skin around the husbands' eyes, flayed
by guilt and promises.
You who risk no more than your own skins
I tell you household gods
are jealous gods.
They will cover your windowsills
with the dust of sunsets;
they will poison your secret wells
with longing.

What We Want

What we want
is never simple.
We move among the things
we thought we wanted:
a face, a room, an open book
and these things bear our names—
now they want us.
But what we want appears
in dreams, wearing disguises.
We fall past,
holding out our arms
and in the morning
our arms ache.
We don't remember the dream,
but the dream remembers us.
It is there all day
as an animal is there
under the table,
as the stars are there
even in full sun.

after minor surgery

this is the dress rehearsal
when the body
like a constant lover
flirts for the first time
with faithlessness

when the body
like a passenger on a long journey
hears the conductor call out
the name
of the first stop

when the body
in all its fear and cunning
makes promises to me
it knows
it cannot keep

Pain

More faithful
than lover or husband
it cleaves to you,
calling itself by your name
as if there had been a ceremony.

At night, you turn and turn
searching for the one
bearable position,
but though you may finally sleep
it wakens ahead of you.

How heavy it is,
displacing with its volume
your very breath.
Before, you seemed to weigh nothing,
your arms might have been wings.

Now each finger adds its measure;
you are pulled down by the weight
of your own hair.
And if your life should disappear ahead of you
you would not run after it.

November

It is an old drama
this disappearance of the leaves,
this seeming death
of the landscape.
In a later scene,
or earlier,
the trees like gnarled magicians
produce handkerchiefs
of leaves
out of empty branches.

And we watch.
We are like children
at this spectacle
of leaves,
as if one day we too
will open the wooden doors
of our coffins
and come out smiling
and bowing
all over again.

Weather Forecast

Somewhere it is about to snow,
if not in the northern suburbs,
then in the west,
if not there, then here.
And the wind
which is camouflaged now
by the perfect stillness of trees
will make some weathercock dizzy
with its fickle breath.
In the blood's failing heat
we wait for the verdict
of snow. You bite into an apple
with the sound boots make
crunching through
the first icy layers.
The whites of your eyes are cold.
The moons of your nails
are frozen mounds.
A single match striking
against the bottom of a shoe
is our only prayer.

blizzard

the snow
has forgotten
how to stop
it falls
stuttering
at the glass
a silk windsock
of snow
blowing
under the porch light
tangling trees
which bend
like old women
snarled
in their own
knitting
snow drifts
up to the step
over the doorsill
a pointillist's blur
the wedding
of form and motion
shaping itself
to the wish of
any object it touches
chairs become
laps of snow
the moon could be
breaking apart
and falling
over the eaves
over the roof
a white bear
shaking its paw
at the window

splitting the hive
of winter
snow stinging
the air
I pull a comforter
of snow
up to my chin
and tumble
to sleep
as the whole
alphabet
of silence
falls out of the
sky

There Are Poems

There are poems
that are never written,
that simply move across
the mind
like skywriting
on a still day:
slowly the first word
drifts west,
the last letters dissolve
on the tongue,
and what is left
is the pure blue
of insight, without cloud
or comfort.

Response

"a ban on the following subject matter:
the Holocaust, grandparents, Friday night
candle lighting . . . Jerusalem at dusk."

—from the poetry editor of *Response*

It is not dusk
in Jerusalem
it is simply morning

and the grandparents have disappeared
into the Holocaust
taking their sabbath candles with them.

Light your poems, hurry.
Already the sun is leaning
towards the west

though the grandparents and candles
have long since burned down
to stubs.

25th Anniversary

There is something I want
to tell you beyond love
or gratitude or sex, beyond
irritation or a purer anger.
For years I have hoarded
your small faults the way
I might hoard kindling
towards some future conflagration,
and from the moment you broke
into my life, all out of breath,
I have half expected you
to break back out.
But here we are
like the married couple
from Cerveteri who smile
from their 6th-century sarcophagus
as if they are giving a party.
How young we were in Rome, buying
their portraits on postcards,
thinking that we too
were entangled already
beyond amputation, beyond
even death, as we are
as we are now.

Ethics

In ethics class so many years ago
our teacher asked this question every fall:
if there were a fire in a museum
which would you save, a Rembrandt painting
or an old woman who hadn't many
years left anyhow? Restless on hard chairs
caring little for pictures or old age
we'd opt one year for life, the next for art
and always half-heartedly. Sometimes
the woman borrowed my grandmother's face
leaving her usual kitchen to wander
some drafty, half-imagined museum.
One year, feeling clever, I replied
why not let the woman decide herself?
Linda, the teacher would report, eschews
the burdens of responsibility.
This fall in a real museum I stand
before a real Rembrandt, old woman,
or nearly so, myself. The colors
within this frame are darker than autumn,
darker even than winter—the browns of earth,
though earth's most radiant elements burn
through the canvas. I know now that woman
and painting and season are almost one
and all beyond saving by children.

from
PM/AM,
1982

◆

Instructions to the Reader

Come. Suspend
willingly or not
your disbelief
and with empty pockets
enter the room
of the story.
Warm your fingers
at this candle
which is only the stub
of a dream
and at any time
may flicker
or go out.
Here fire consumes
itself
with paper
and pencil for kindling;
here a unicorn waits
in the corner
its musical horn
ready.
When I tell you
this story is pure fact
you will want to leave
the room.
Stay awhile.
Evil is simply
a grammatical error:
a failure to leap
the precipice
between "he"
and "I."
There is also a beggar here
with a bowl of rice.
Fill your pockets,

hurry,
of the thousands of nights
there are only
a handful left.
At the end
the typesetter
will distribute
the type.
The letters will be divided
from all meaning,
separate as stars
whose small teeth chatter
but make no sense.
Only thus
is sleep possible.

PM

The child is unreconciled
to the dark. Adrift
on her small bed
she listens
for voices down the hall
as if they were familiar waves
lapping at the unknown shore.
But her mother is almost silent.
The needle has dropped
from her hand,
and the only embroidery left
is the sky
stretched between window frames.
Her father loosens his tie.
He has used up
his small store of words,
and even his sleep will be burdened
by the heavy breathing of others.
This is how she remembers it:
the house creaking
as if it were loose
on its moorings;
the unnavigable dark.

AM

The child gets up
on the wrong side of the bed.
There are splinters
of cold light on the floor,
and when she frowns
the frown freezes on her face
as her mother has warned her it would.
When she puts her elbows roughly
on the table her father says:
you got up on the wrong side of the bed;
and there is suddenly
a cold river
of spilled milk.
These gestures are merely formal,
small stitches in the tapestry
of a childhood she will remember
as nearly happy. Outside
the snow begins again,
ordinary weather
blurring the landscape
between that time and this,
as she swings her cold legs
over the side of the bed.

A Name

for Susan who became Shoshana

David means beloved.
Peter is a rock. They named me
Linda which means beautiful
in Spanish—a language
I never learned.
Even naked
we wear our names.
In the end we leave them behind
carved into desktops
and gravestones, inscribed
on the flyleaf of Bibles
where on another page
God names the generations
of Shem, Ham, and Japheth.

Homer cast a spell with names
giving us the list
of warriors and their ships
I read my children to sleep by.
There are as many names underfoot
as leaves in October;
they burn as briefly on the tongue,
and their smoke could darken
the morning sky to dusk.
Remember the boy of seven
who wandered the Holocaust alone
and lost not his life
but his name? Or the prince whose name
was stolen with his kingdom?

When I took my husband's name
and fastened it to mine
I was as changed
as a child

when the priest sprinkles it
with water and the name
that saves it a place in heaven.
My grandfather gave me a name
in Hebrew I never heard,
but it died with him.
If I had taken that name
who would I be,
and if he calls me now
how will I know to answer?

The Printer

for R. H.

Baskerville, Perpetua, Garamond:
I thought you were naming a dance,
but the only minuet is typeface moving
across the page, and you in your apron bowing—
journeyman to the letter, apprentice to the word.
The smell of ink, like the smell of bread
signifies morning, a bleeding of color
at the horizon, the horizon itself
a line of boldface too distant to read.

In this world there are as many letters
as leaves, as birds, as flecks of ash
whole armies of alphabets march across
margins of pavement, margins of snow.
Now there's a smudge on your forehead
where your hand strayed
making those architectural gestures,
the Pleasure of our Company is requested,
the ceremonial announcement of birth or death.

Your press is as fruitful as a wine press,
the sound of its motion like surf, hour after hour
reams of paper spreading their deckle-edged foam.
At night you distribute the type as carefully
as if you were placing your daughters in their beds.
Dark enters, a time before language,
but the sky is printed in white indelible stars,
with God's own signature—that thumbprint of moon,
like the printer's colophon
on heaviest Mohawk Superfine.

Detail from the Altarpiece at Ghent

The angels
in the corner
crowd this postcard,
ready to fly
wherever the mails
might take them.

They have the scrubbed faces
and the gauzy hair
of my daughter's friends
in high school chorus,
their cupped mouths brimming
with hallelujahs.

Wrapped in the reds
and golds of cherubim
those rough girls too
dreamed about boys,
and when van Eyck was done
grew up and married them

and died. Today I pin
their picture to my wall
where the bronze notes
of the sun's great harp
can strike them
back to song.

Mosaic

1. THE SACRIFICE

On this tile
the knife
like a sickle-moon hangs
in the painted air
as if it had learned a dance
of its own,
the way the boy has
among the vivid
breakable flowers,
the way Abraham has
among the boulders,
his two feet heavy
as stones.

2. NEAR SINAI

God's hand here
is the size of a tiny cloud,
and the wordless tablets
he holds out
curve like the temple doors.
Moses, reaching up
must see on their empty surface
laws chiseled in his mind
by the persistent wind
of the desert, by wind
in the bulrushes.

3. THE FLIGHT INTO EGYPT

We know by the halos
that circle these heads
like rings around planets
that the small donkey

has carried his burden
away from the thunder
of the Old Testament
into the lightning
of the New.

4. AT THE ARMENIAN TILE SHOP

Under the bright glazes
Esau watches Jacob,
Cain watches Abel.
With the same heavy eyes
the tilemaker's Arab assistant
watches me,
all of us wondering
why for every pair
there is just one
blessing.

Ark

"The wooden coffer containing the tables of the law
kept in the Holiest Place of the Tabernacle . . ."

—*Oxford English Dictionary*

for Stephen and Elizabeth

We all know
how the animals entered
that other ark
in twos,
even the promiscuous rooster
with his chosen hen,
even the snakes entwined,
remembering an earlier voyage
from Eden.
And Noah himself who knew
the worst of matrimony,
bitter words for breakfast,
complaints of sawdust
on the floor, nails underfoot;
at night her back turned
hard and cold as the tablets.
Later the calls of mating
through the wet nights,
the tiny whir
of the hummingbirds' twin motors,
the monkeys' odd duet.
When the dove flew off
to find land
its mate perched on the railing,
the only creature
in that windy world alone.
I remember my wedding.
Standing before the ark
I thought of seas of matrimony,

of shipwreck.
When he stepped on the glass,
to recall the ruined temple, they say,
I whispered: Man's dominion
over Woman. He smiled and shook his head
and later held a shard of glass
up to the light. In it
we saw condensed a perfect rainbow
and the white flash
of the dove's return.

Lists

I made a list of things I have
to remember and a list
of things I want to forget,
but I see they are the same list.
I made a list of items of need:
love and water on one side,
on the other the small flowers
that bloom without scent,
and it is like the grocery lists
my grandmother used to make:
milk and butter—dairy
on one side, meat on the other
as if they shouldn't mingle
even on the page.
My mother makes lists on tiny
scraps of paper, leaving them
on chairs or the seats of the bus
the way she drops a handkerchief
for someone to find, a clue
a kind of commerce between her
and the world.
And all the time the tree
is making its endless list
of leaves; the sky
is listing its valuables
in rain. My daughter
lists the books she means to read,
and their names are like the exotic
names of birds on my husband's
life list. Perhaps God
listed what to create
in a week: earth and oceans,
the armature of heaven
with a place to fasten

every star, and finally
Adam who rested a day
then made a list of his own:
starling, deer, and serpent.

In the Middle of a Life

Tonight I understand
for the first time
how a woman might choose
her own death
as easily
as if it were a dark plum
she picked
from a basket
of bright peaches.

It wouldn't be despair
that moved her
or hunger,
but a kind of stillness.
The evenings are full
of closure: the pale flowers
of the shamrock fold
their fragile wings, everything
promised has been given.

There is always
that moment
when the sun balanced
on the rim
of the world
falls
and is lost at sea,
and the sky seems huge
and beautiful without it.

I lie down on my bed
giving myself
to the white sheets
as the white sheets of a sloop
must give themselves
to the wind,
setting out on a journey—
the last perhaps,
or even the first.

Water Wheel

1.

Afraid of sleep
the child asks
for one more drink of water.

2.

You hold my face between your two hands
as steadily as if I were a cup
about to spill.

3.

Remember this morning how the ocean's edge
unraveled at our feet, tangling us
in its accidental lace?

4.

You said we know what water is
although we never swim
in other oceans.

5.

Sometimes I dream of sitting in a waterfall,
of letting it churn like white fur
over my naked shoulders.

6.

It was fidelity you meant,
the stillness at the center
of the whirlpool.

7.

The waves are taking
our island inch by inch,
an army that will overrun us soon.

8.

You want a life
as simple as a cup
of rain,

9.

but see
how my reflection wavers
even in this glass.

10.

I think you'd throw cold water
in my face
to wash temptation out.

11.

The waterfalls
of sleep tumble
over us.

12.

I ask
for one more icy sip
of water.

from
A FRACTION OF DARKNESS,
1985

◆

Overture

This is the way it begins: the small
sure voice of the woodwind
leads us down a path brocaded
with colored leaves, deep
into a forest we almost remember.
And though the percussions
have no exact equivalent,
soon we will find ourselves
thinking of weather—
a cold front rumbling in—
or of applause, not for the self
but for someone we watch
bowing at the edge
of a pond whose waters,
like the cello's darkest waters, part
letting the melody
slip through. This theme
presents itself so shyly
that when it returns full grown,
though it plucks
the live nerve of recollection
we will hear it
as if for the first time.
Make no mistake, this is only
music, shading with evening
into a minor key.
Whole flocks of birds rush up
spreading their night wings
as the harpist, that angel
who guarded the gates
in strict black, sweeps
her arm from E to G to high C,
and the bowing stranger
lifts his wand, letting
the curtains part.

In the Kingdom of Midas

If you follow the sun
from room to room,
wading in the pools
of light spilled
by that tawny,
molten river,

if you move all day
from east
to west, from kitchen
to study to bed,
by afternoon you'll see
the bedposts touched

and changed to sheaves of wheat,
and the children born
and nourished there will be
golden tongued
and golden headed.

For you the moon has always been
the pale,
homely sister.
You tell your rosary
in saffron beads of light,

and though one day
you'll drown
in shade, the sun
will leave its heavy coins
on your closed lids
forever.

Suffocation

for R. J. P.

In Chekhov's *Three Sisters,* everyone
is infected with terminal boredom.
When Irena says her soul is like a locked
piano without a key, I want
to tell her that playing the piano too
the fingers can wander up and down
the scales, going nowhere.
And when the talk leads always back
to Moscow, where she longs to be,
I wish I could remind Olga of the cold,
unyielding streets where even the ice hardens
to the color of stone. Sitting here, watching
someone I love slowly die, I see
how anguish and boredom can be married
for years, an ill-assorted couple, suffocating
in each other's arms. I watched Masha
at the curtain call, the tears still streaming
down her face as she moved from one self
to the other through the wall
of applause, a kind of backwards birth.
And I wondered where all that feeling
came from if not some deep pool
where one can be dragged and dragged
beneath the surface but never quite drown.
Russia . . . I thought, Russia . . . a country
my grandfather thought he had escaped from
but which he wore always
like the heavy overcoat in the story
by Gogol, or the overcoat he wrapped me in
one night when the grown-ups kept on talking,
and I shivered and yawned in an ecstasy
of boredom that made my childhood
seem a vast continent I could only escape from
hidden in a coat, in steerage, and at great risk.

Japanese Lantern

After dreaming for years
over the black and white pages
of Katsura Palace,
we ordered a stone lantern
from Japan
and placed it in the garden
among American hollies
and an Austrian pine.
Next spring we'll prune the pine
the Japanese way, snipping
the clusters of new growth
that are like the short, stiff brooms
that Japanese women use
to clear Katsura's paths.
Tonight outlined in snow
our path is Japanese.
An animal has wandered by
leaving its tracks like ideographs
we cannot read,
although they lead somewhere
deep and familiar
in our woods.
Even these trees are textured
like the tree trunks
in the woodblock print
we hung over the bed. The eye is led
down needled paths
to a lantern almost like ours
with two lit windows.
At one a woman loosens her kimono.
At the other a man bends
over a book—Katsura perhaps,
where from the moon-viewing platform
something the size
of an almond can be seen

aslant in the sky.
When the lantern goes out
that moon will be broken
into a thousand fragments
and translated here
as snow.

Realms of Gold

1. RECESS

I used to think
the cover of a book
was a door I could pull shut
after me,
that I was as safe
between pages
as between the clean sheets
of my bed at home.
The children in those books
were not like me.
They had the shine
of bravery or luck,
and their stories had endings.
But when Miss Colton called
"Yoo Hoo, Third Grade,"
and I had to come running,
the book suddenly
slippery under my arm, sometimes
those children ran with me.

2. THE QUARREL

"What are you doing,"
he asks, and I turn a page,
then another.
"Are you still reading?"
And I pile page
after page, like sandbags,
between us.
I'm going to tear
that book out of your hands,
he says, but I don't hear him,
the sound of pages turning
is like a far train approaching,

and Anna has just
entered the station.

3. FINAL INSTRUCTIONS

When the time comes,
make my grave
with clean sheets
and a comforter of flowers.
If you come to call, rest
against the stone
which will lean
like a bookend
over my head.
Make yourself
at home there.
Read to me!

Prosody 101

When they taught me that what mattered most
was not the strict iambic line goose-stepping
over the page but the variations
in that line and the tension produced
on the ear by the surprise of difference,
I understood yet didn't understand
exactly, until just now, years later
in spring, with the trees already lacy
and camellias blowsy with middle age
I looked out and saw what a cold front had done
to the garden, sweeping in like common language,
unexpected in the sensuous
extravagance of a Maryland spring.
There was a dark edge around each flower
as if it had been outlined in ink
instead of frost, and the tension I felt
between the expected and actual
was like that time I came to you, ready
to say goodbye for good, for you had been
a cold front yourself lately, and as I walked in
you laughed and lifted me up in your arms
as if I too were lacy with spring
instead of middle-aged like the camellias,
and I thought: So this is Poetry.

Orpheus

When Orpheus turned
and looked back and knew
that genius wasn't enough,
I wonder which he regretted most:
the failure of will,
Eurydice lost,
or what it must mean for her
to remain
a fraction of darkness?

Did he still tame animals
with his songs,
or would that seem a child's game now?
Did he tune his lyre
to a minor key,
the last notes falling
like darkened leaves
to drift towards Lesbos?

In Balanchine's ballet
the failure seems Eurydice's fault
who tempted his blindfold off,
as if the artist must be absolved,
as if what matters
is the body itself—
that instrument stringed
with tendon and bone
making its own music.

Green Thumb

No bigger than a thumb
and palest green,
a tree frog
has stowed away
on one of the plants
my husband brought inside
for winter, and in the darkness
it fills the spaces
of this house
with disproportionate
song. The dogs bark,
fearing a creature
they cannot see,
and partly to quiet them
we search in vain
among the stems
and roots and leaves
for that balloon
of swollen sound—
either lovelorn,
or joyful, or hungry.
I'm never sure
I want the woods inside,
though circumscribed in pots
these plants seem safe enough—
contained explosions of green
at every frozen window.
Whatever my husband touches
grows. Tonight when he
touches me, black earth
still rings the moons
of all his nails. I think
it is a naked infant's call
the tree frog's song
reminds me of.

Dream Plants

You give me fuchsias for my birthday,
their strange bell-like flowers
improbable shades of red,
the color of Buddhist temple bells.
These are dream plants—not quite nightmares
but those shadowy dreams left over from childhood
where terror and beauty mix
and the difference between plants and animals
is vaguer than we thought.

For your birthday I give books
I hope to read when you are finished,
though I know you'd rather be out
in the garden planting
than reading books.
I think gardens are for reading in,
a kind of background to please the eye
as the pages turn—a pause in mid-sentence
brief as a comma. So we try to give

our own lives to each other, to change
places a moment in the slow dance through time.
The plants you give me will make their way
to your desk; the books will be left
on my side of the bed. And we will look
at each other with an old promise
improbable as the reds of the fuchsias
or the intricate terror and beauty
I look for in books.

Nostalgia

At the moment when memory dims
a whole octave, when the light
it throws backwards
becomes soft, a powdery light
blurring
the eye and dulling
the sharp blade of feeling—
at that moment we relinquish
our childhoods.

My dead father stands waving.
He has forgotten all my failures,
and under his black mustache surely he smiles.
My mother has left her mirror
and stands by the stove.
Around her cluster the sisters
and brothers I never had, though I leaned
out of an open window for years
calling their names.

Let the bare bones of fact
beat their terrible rhythms
elsewhere. On the Grand Concourse
the Bronx Bus stopped
and started all night,
but I only remember
a faithful beast
breathing
over my broken sleep.

Market Day

We have traveled all this way
to see the real France:
these trays of apricots and grapes spilled out
like semi-precious stones
for us to choose; a milky way
of cheeses whose names like planets
I forget; heraldic sole
displayed on ice, as if the fish
themselves had just escaped,
leaving their scaled armor behind.
There's nothing like this
anywhere, you say. And I see
Burnside Avenue in the Bronx, my mother

sending me for farmer cheese and lox:
the rounds of cheese grainy and white, pocked
like the surface of the moon;
the silken slices of smoked fish
lying in careful pleats; and always,
as here, sawdust under our feet
the color of sand brought in on pant cuffs
from Sunday at the beach.
Across the street on benches,
my grandparents lifted their faces
to the sun the way the blind turn
towards a familiar sound, speaking
another language I almost understand.

Family Scene: Mid-Twentieth Century

In the photograph you and I sit together
with identical smiles,
each holding a dog by the collar;
the ocean is simply backdrop.
Marriage, could be the caption,
which frees and confines at the same time,
as those leashless dogs, now dead
were checked by our hands on their collars.
It is probably just coincidence
that I found this photograph pressed
between pages of Tolstoy, though
I always said that you looked Russian—
Levin, I suppose, not Vronsky, with your passion
for land and for growing.
Someone will find this picture
years from now and think:
mid-twentieth century, family scene,
people had pets instead of children.
Though of course we had children too
off somewhere, swimming perhaps
in that backdrop of water.
Who were we smiling for, ten years ago,
and what can we believe
if not our own faces in photos?
When you want to go faster, go slower!
a poet said, speaking of running marathons.
I want to go slower now, seeing only
darkness ahead, but you always hurry me on.
Didn't you rush us into this life together,
almost without thinking,
or at least holding our thoughts
the way we might hold our breath?
And didn't it all work out? you ask,
for there we are, twenty years into our marathon
caught in black and white and smiling,

and here we are now.
Dumb luck, my father would have said,
who never quite approved of you.
But who can ask for anything more of life
than those strategies of the genes
or the weather which we call luck?

September

it rained in my sleep
and in the morning the fields were wet

I dreamed of artillery
of the thunder of horses

in the morning the fields were strewn
with twigs and leaves

as if after a battle
or a sudden journey

I went to sleep in summer
I dreamed of rain

in the morning the fields were wet
and it was autumn

Routine Mammogram

We are looking for a worm
in the apple—
that fruit which ever since Eden

has been susceptible
to frost
or appetite.

The doctor shows me
aerial photographs,
moonscapes

of craters and lakes,
faults in the surface
I might fall through one day

valleys where every shadow
could mean total
eclipse.

This is just a baseline, he says
as if my body were a camp
you could start climbing from.

In the mountains
they dream of snow and listen
for avalanche.

I think of Amazon women
with just one
breast,

their bowstrings
tightening
for war.

(How will we
ever
touch again?)

You're fine, the doctor
tells me now and smiles,
as if he could give innocence back,

as if he could give back
to the apple
its spiraled skin.

Departures

They seemed to all take off
at once: Aunt Grace
whose kidneys closed shop;
Cousin Rose who fed sugar
to diabetes;
my grandmother's friend
who postponed going so long
we thought she'd stay.

It was like the summer years ago
when they all set out on trains
and ships, wearing hats with veils
and the proper gloves,
because everybody was going
someplace that year,
and they didn't want
to be left behind.

Duet for One Voice

I sit at your side
watching the tides of consciousness
move in and out, watching
the nurses, their caps
like so many white gulls circling
the bed. The window
grows slowly dark,
and light again,
and dark. The clock
tells the same old stories.
Last week you said, now
you'll have to learn
to sew for yourself.
If the thread is boredom,
the needle is grief.
I sit here learning.

2.

In place of spring
I offer this branch
of forsythia
whose yellow blossoms
I have forced.
Your tired mouth
forces a smile
in thanks. Outside
it is still cold;
who knows how long
the cold will last?
But underground,
their banners still furled,
whole armies of flowers wait.

3.

I am waiting for you to die,
even as I try to coax you
back to life
with custards and soup
and colored pills I shake
from the bottle like dice,
though their magic
went out of the world
with my surgeon father,
the last magician.
I am waiting

for you to be again
what you always were,
for you to be there whole
for me to run to with this new grief—
your death—the hair grown back
on your skull the way it used to be,
your widow's peak the one sure landmark
on the map of my childhood,
those years when I believed
that medicine and love and being good
could save us all.

4.

We escape from our mothers
again and again, young
Houdinis, playing the usual matinees.
First comes escape down
the birth canal, our newly carved faces
leading the way like figureheads
on ancient slaveships,
our small hands rowing for life.
Later escape into silence, escape
behind slammed doors,

the flight into marriage.
I thought I was finally old enough
to sit with you, sharing a book.
But when I look up
from the page, you
have escaped from me.

The Death of a Parent

Move to the front
of the line
a voice says, and suddenly
there is nobody
left standing between you
and the world, to take
the first blows
on their shoulders.
This is the place in books
where part one ends, and
part two begins,
and there is no part three.
The slate is wiped
not clean but like a canvas
painted over in white
so that a whole new landscape
must be started,
bits of the old
still showing underneath—
those colors sadness lends
to a certain hour of evening.
Now the line of light
at the horizon
is the hinge between earth
and heaven, only visible
a few moments
as the sun drops
its rusted padlock
into place.

Shadows

Each night this house sinks into the shadows
under its weight of love and fear and pity.
Each morning it floats up again so lightly
it seems attached to sky instead of earth,
a place where we will always go on living
and there will be no dead to leave behind.

But when we think of whom we've left behind
already in the ever-hungry shadows,
even in the morning hum of living
we pause a minute and are filled with pity
for the lovely children of the earth
who run up and down the stairs so lightly

and who weave their careless songs so lightly
through the hedges which they play behind
that the fruits and flowers of the earth
rise up on their stems above the shadows.
Perhaps even an apple can feel pity;
perhaps the lilac wants to go on living.

In this house where we have all been living
we bind the family together lightly
with knots made equally of love and pity
and the knowledge that we'll leave behind
only partial memories, scraps of shadows,
trinkets of our years upon the earth.

I think about my father in the earth
as if it were a room in which he's living,
as if it were a house composed of shadows
where he remembers those he loved not lightly,
where he remembers what he left behind.
He had a great capacity for pity

but told me that I mustn't waste my pity
on him—he'd had his share of life on earth,
and he was happy just to leave behind
daughters of daughters who would go on living.
So he seemed to leave us almost lightly,
closing the curtains which were stitched with shadows.

Always save your pity for the living
who walk the eggshell crust of earth so lightly,
in front of them, behind them, only shadows.

from

THE IMPERFECT PARADISE,
1988

◆

Grudnow

When he spoke of where he came from,
my grandfather could have been
clearing his throat
of that name, that town
sometimes Poland, sometimes Russia,
the borders pencilled in
with a hand as shaky as his.
He left, I heard him say,
because there was nothing there.

I understood what he meant
when I saw the photograph
of his people standing
against a landscape emptied
of crops and trees, scraped raw
by winter. Everything
was in sepia, as if the brown earth
had stained the faces,
stained even the air.

I would have died there, I think
in childhood maybe
of some fever,
my face pressed for warmth
against a cow with flanks
like those of the great aunts
in the picture. Or later
I would have died of history
like the others, who dug

their stubborn heels into that earth,
heels as hard as the heels
of the bread my grandfather tore
from the loaf at supper. He always
sipped his tea through a cube of sugar

clenched in his teeth, the way
he sipped his life here, noisily,
through all he remembered
that might have been sweet in Grudnow.

To a Daughter Leaving Home

When I taught you
at eight to ride
a bicycle, loping along
beside you
as you wobbled away
on two round wheels,
my own mouth rounding
in surprise when you pulled
ahead down the curved
path of the park,
I kept waiting
for the thud
of your crash as I
sprinted to catch up,
while you grew
smaller, more breakable
with distance,
pumping, pumping
for your life, screaming
with laughter,
the hair flapping
behind you like a
handkerchief waving
goodbye.

The Dogwoods

I remember, in the week
of the dogwoods, why sometimes
we give up everything
for beauty, lose our sense
and our senses, as we do now
for these blossoms, sprinkled
like salt through the dark woods.

And like the story of pheasants
with salt on their tails
to tame them,
look how we are made helpless
by a brief explosion
of petals
one week in April.

After an Absence

After an absence that was no one's fault
we are shy with each other,
and our words seem younger than we are,
as if we must return to the time we met
and work ourselves back to the present,
the way you never read a story
from the place you stopped
but always start each book all over again.
Perhaps we should have stayed
tied like mountain climbers
by the safe cord of the phone,
its dial our own small prayer wheel,
our voices less ghostly across the miles,
less awkward than they are now.
I had forgotten the grey in your curls,
that splash of winter over your face,
remembering the younger man
you used to be.

And I feel myself turn old and ordinary,
having to think again of food for supper,
the animals to be tended, the whole riptide
of daily life hidden but perilous
pulling both of us under so fast.
I have dreamed of our bed
as if it were a shore where we would be washed up,
not this striped mattress
we must cover with sheets. I had forgotten
all the old business between us,
like mail unanswered so long that silence
becomes eloquent, a message of its own.
I had even forgotten how married love
is a territory more mysterious

the more it is explored, like one of those terrains
you read about, a garden in the desert
where you stoop to drink, never knowing
if your mouth will fill with water or sand.

In the Rearview Mirror

Driving all night in winter,
I watch in the rearview mirror
as the small towns disappear
behind us, ceasing
to exist the moment
we pass. Hills rise and fall
brindled with snow,
and in the fields a few
lit windows small
as night-lights
remind us of a child asleep
upstairs, the blanket rising
and falling with his breath.
How the particular
loses itself. Downstairs
the dough is rising
under its cloth, and the Mother
whose hands have learned
the wisdom of kneading
touches the Father.
And one town dims
and flickers out, and another
stirs ready to rise
three hundred miles later
when the sun touches the farthest edge
of the sky in an endless
relay race of light,
at a place half resurrected
from childhood and waiting
to be unwrapped like a withheld gift
from the white ribbon
of unwinding road.

At the Loom

You sit at the loom,
your hands raised
like silhouetted birds,
or like a harpist poised
at the strings of an instrument
whose chords are colors,
their slow accumulation,
thread by thread—
a kind of bleeding upward
the way the sky bleeds
from the horizon up
after certain sunsets.
Monk's belt and rosepath . . .
plainweave and twill . . .
The shuttle moves back
and forth, trailing
its wake of yarn
as if by accident,
and patterns that seem
random at first multiply
into beauty.
No wonder Penelope burned
with patience.
Somewhere a sheep bleats
in the night, a silkworm
stirs in its cocoon.
You weave a spell,
I wear it on my back,
and though the chilly stars
go bone naked
we are clothed.

Rereading *The Odyssey* in Middle Age

Why was she weaving a shroud for Laertes
and why have I thought for years
it was a shawl she made, something warm
a man might wrap around her shoulders
windy nights—one of the suitors, perhaps,
much younger than she
and younger far than Odysseus.
Perhaps Laertes kept his eye on her
suspiciously. Did she mean
to finish it after all, unweaving
less and less each night, and could that mean
she wished Laertes dead? Yarns dyed the colors
of the sea: greens, purples, and hyacinth.
How can we hope to find the darker threads
of her impatience or lust
in the design of that nubby material?
We make our myths from whole cloth anyway
and make ourselves the heroines
of others' imaginings.

The shuttle was always moving back
and forth across the loom, as restless
as Odysseus himself, or any man.
I think of the uses of "shroud":
how the night can be shrouded in fog
in places like this one, near the sea;
how leaves in summer shroud each mother branch;
and how your husband's father looks at you
with wrinkled lids shrouding
those knowing eyes.
What is faithfulness anyway?
Penelope asks. Is the sea faithful
to the shore, whether it beats against it
or withdraws, leaving only a trace
of its commandment on the naked sand?

She wonders if Telemachus will find a wife
to weave a shroud for her lost
father-in-law, or would the water
be winding sheet enough for him?

Circe

I will always be the other woman.
I disappear
for a time
like the moon in daylight,
then rise at night all mother-of-pearl
so that a man's upturned face,
watching,
will have reflected on it
the milk of longing.

And though he may leave, memory
will perfect me.
One day the light
may fall in a certain way
on Penelope's hair,
and he will pause wildly . . .
but when she turns,
it will only be his wife, to whom
white sheets simply mean laundry—

even Nausikaa
in her silly braids
thought more of washing linen
than of him,
preferring Odysseus
clean and oiled
to that briny,
unkempt lion
I would choose.

Let Dido and her kind
leap from cliffs
for love.
My men will moan and dream of me
for years . . .

desire and need
become the same animal
in the silken
dark.

To be the other woman
is to be a season
that is always about to end,
when the air is flowered
with jasmine and peach,
and the weather day after day
is flawless,
and the forecast
is hurricane.

The Sirens

Is there no music now
except the chime
of coins in the pocket
for which a man would go breathlessly
off course, would even drown?
Odysseus tied to his mast
regretted his own foresight.

In ordinary days to come in Ithaca
the song of some distant bird,
the chords of water against
the shore, even Penelope
humming to herself at the loom
would make his head turn, his eyes
stray toward the sea.

The Safecracker

On nights when the moon seems impenetrable—
a locked porthole to space;
when the householder bars his windows
and doors, and his dog lies until dawn,
one jeweled eye open; when the maiden sleeps
with her rosy knees sealed tightly together,
on such nights the safecracker sets to work.
Axe . . . Chisel . . . Nitroglycerin . . .
Within the vault lie forty thousand
tons of gold; the heaped up spoils
of Ali Baba's cave; the secrets of the molecule.
He sands his fingertips
to feel the subtle vibrations
of wheel lining up, just so, with wheel.
His toolmarks are his fingerprints.
And now a crack appears on the side
of the egg, a single fault line,
and within: the golden yolk just waiting.
A kind of wind . . . a door flies open . . . a glitter
of forsythia forced out of the branch.
With smoothest fingertips you touch
the locked cage of my ribs . . . just so.
My knees fall open. And Cleopatra smiles,
whose own Egyptians first invented the lock.

Ars Poetica

1. THE MUSE

You may catch
a butterfly
in a net
if you are swift enough

or if you keep
perfectly still
perhaps it will land
on your shoulder.

Often
it is just
a moth.

2. WRITING

In the battle
between the typewriter
and the blank page
a certain rhythm evolves,
not unlike the hoofbeats
of a horse groomed for war
who would rather be
head down, grazing.

3. REJECTION SLIP

Darling, though you know
I admire your many
fine qualities
you don't fill all my needs
just now, and besides
there's a backlog
waiting to fit
in my bed.

4. REVISION

The tree has been green
all summer, but now
it tries red . . . copper . . .
even gold. Soon
leaf after leaf
will be discarded,
there will be nothing
but bare tree, soon
it will be almost time
to start over again.

5. ARS POETICA

Escape from the poem
by bus, by streetcar—
any way you can,
dragging a suitcase
tied together with twine
in which you've stuffed
all your singular belongings.

Leave behind
a room
washed by sun
or moonlight.
There should be a chair
on which you've draped a coat
that will fit anyone.

The Ordinary Weather of Summer

In the ordinary weather of summer,
with storms rumbling from west to east
like so many freight trains hauling
their cargo of heat and rain,
the dogs sprawl on the back steps, panting,
insects assemble at every window,
and we quarrel again, bombarding
each other with small grievances,
our tempers flashing on and off
in bursts of heat lightning.
In the cooler air of morning,
we drink our coffee amicably enough
and walk down to the sea
which seems to tremble with meaning
and into which we plunge again and again.
The days continue hot.
At dusk the shadows are as blue
as the lips of the children stained
with berries or with the chill
of too much swimming.
So we move another summer closer
to our last summer together—
a time as real and implacable as the sea
out of which we come walking
on wobbly legs as if for the first time,
drying ourselves with rough towels,
shaking the water out of our blinded eyes.

A Walk before Breakfast

Isn't this what life
could be: a walk
before breakfast with the sea
opening its chapters
of water and light,
flexing its silken muscle,
pulsing back and forth—
a kind of accompaniment
to breath? Along its rough edges
shells and small birds gather,
the rick-rack of life
in all its stages: feather
and fish bone, those sand crabs
that we see only by their tiny
pinpricks of absence.
All summer we eat when the tug
of appetite tells us,
make love at odd moments,
the sand beneath us
as pliant as flesh.
If we refused to leave,
would our skins turn
the amber of beer glass?
Would we learn to walk always arched
into the wind, half naked
and vulnerable and tough
as seaweed, leaving behind
not footprints
but the discarded carapace
of our other life?

Erosion

We are slowly
undermined. Grain
by grain . . .
inch by inch . . .
slippage.
It happens as we watch.
The waves move their long row
of scythes over the beach.

It happens as we sleep,
the way the clock's hands
move continuously
just out of sight,
but more like an hourglass
than a clock,
for here sand
is running out.

We wake to water.
Implacably lovely
is this view
though it will swallow
us whole, soon
there will be
nothing left
but view.

We have tried a seawall.
we have tried prayer.
We have planted grasses
on the bank, small tentacles,
hooks of green that catch
on nothing. For the wind
does its work, the water
does its sure work.

One day the sea will simply
take us. The children
press their faces to the glass
as if the windows were portholes,
and the house fills
with animals: two dogs,
a bird, cats—we are becoming
an ark already.

The gulls will follow
our wake.
We are made of water anyway,
I can feel it in the yielding
of your flesh, though sometimes
I think that you are sand,
moving slowly, slowly
from under me.

Snowing: A Triptych

1.

It is snowing
so lightly
the air seems blurred
with static
through which I see white
rimming the woods
like shadows on the negatives
of old pictures.
Only the cardinals flame
out of the trees
with the hard-edged
purposes
of hunger.

2.

This is pure
process,
the blinding
imperative
of physics
or art,
as a billion
anonymous
crystals—each
an artisan of light,
hurl
through the cold
air.

3.

I want to be buried
like this,
the snow falling
and falling
into the earth
until every crevice
and canyon
is filled,
as in China
when for burial
they filled the seven
openings
of the body
with white
jade.

Family Tree

How many leaves
has death undone already
poplar   maple   oak

raked into funeral pyres
and burned
gathered

in empty sacks
and dragged away
larch   linden   birch

leaves like the maps
of small countries
I will never visit

palm-shaped leaves
whose life lines
have run out?

How many leaves
in the long autumn retreat
their brown uniforms crisp

has the wind
taken away
or scattered

like drying shells
at the edge
of a grassy surf

cherry   sumac   elm
tear-shaped or
burned out stars

while the trunks
of the trees grow fat
and the branches shake?

I stand on a New Year's Day
unwilling to drink
to a year

that will bring me
one new life
but take another back

and I count
the leaves
walnut   ash

the chorus
of silent throats
telling again

and again
the long story
of smoke.

The Deathwatch Beetle

1.

A cardinal hurls itself
at my window all morning long,
trying so hard to penetrate
its own reflection
I almost let it in myself,
though once I saw
another red bird, crazed
by the walls of a room,
spatter its feathers
all over the house.

2.

My whole childhood is coming apart,
the last stitches
about to be ripped out
with your death,
and I will be left—ridiculous,
to write
condolence letters
to myself.

3.

The deathwatch beetle
earned its name
not from its ugliness
or our terror
of insects
but simply because of the sound
it makes, ticking.

4.

When your spirit
perfects itself,
will it escape
out of a nostril,
or through the spiral
passage of an ear?
Or is it even now battering
against your thin skull, wild
to get through, blood brother
to this crimson bird?

Elegy

Last night the moon lifted itself
on one wing
over the fields

and struggling to rise
this morning
like a hooked fish

through watery
layers
of sleep,

I know
with what difficulty
flowers

must pull themselves
all the way up
their stems.

How much easier
the free fall of snow
or leaves in their season.

All week, watching
the hospital gown
rising

and falling
with your raggedy breath,
I dreamed

not of resurrections
but of the slow, sensual
slide each night

into sleep, of dust
or newly shovelled earth
settling.

Something about the Trees

I remember what my father told me:
There is an age when you are most yourself.
He was just past fifty then,
Was it something about the trees that made him speak?

There is an age when you are most yourself.
I know more now than I did once.
Was it something about the trees that made him speak?
Only a single leaf had turned so far.

I know more now than I did once.
I used to think he'd always be the surgeon.
Only a single leaf had turned so far.
Even his body kept its secrets.

I used to think he'd always be the surgeon,
My mother was the perfect surgeon's wife.
Even his body kept its secrets.
I thought they both would live forever.

My mother was the perfect surgeon's wife,
I still can see her face at thirty.
I thought they both would live forever,
I thought I'd always be their child.

I still can see her face at thirty.
When will I be most myself?
I thought I'd always be their child.
In my sleep it's never winter.

When will I be most myself?
I remember what my father told me.
In my sleep it's never winter.
He was just past fifty then.

Fruit of the Tree

There were so many
kinds of fruit in that garden:
grapes and nectarines, plums
swelling out of their very skins,
kiwis whose ridiculous
name they had chosen, laughing.

But the apple was the color
of a hunter's moon
in whose light
it glowed as if lit up
from within.
The apple

was a mystery begging
to be solved.
Never mind the serpent.
Adam was off raking.
Eve would be the mother
of Newton and Bohr.

Years later
stockpiled in barns,
an apple could explode inward,
releasing the smell
of the whole
dying year.

Mother Eve

Of course she never was a child herself,
waking as she did one morning
full grown and perfect,
with only Adam, another innocent,
to love her and instruct.
There was no learning, step by step,
to walk, no bruised elbows or knees—
no small transgressions.
There was only the round, white mound
of the moon rising,
which could neither be suckled
nor leaned against.
And perhaps the serpent spoke
in a woman's voice, mothering.
Oh, who can blame her?

When she held her own child
in her arms, what did she make
of that new animal? Did she love Cain
too little or too much, looking down
at her now flawed body as if her rib,
like Adam's, might be gone?
In the litany of naming that continued
for children instead of plants,
no daughter is mentioned.
But generations later there was Rachel,
all mother herself, who knew
that bringing forth a child in pain
is only the start. It is losing them
(and Benjamin so young)
that is the punishment.

On the Question of Free Will

Sometimes,
noticing the skeleton
embossed
on every leaf

and how
the lion's mouth
and antelope's neck
fit perfectly,

I wonder
at God's plan
had Eve refused
the apple.

The Animals

When I see a suckling pig turn
on the spit, its mouth around
an apple, or feel the soft
muzzle of a horse
eating a windfall from my hand,
I think about the animals
when Eden closed down,
who stole no fruit themselves.

After feeding so long
from Adam's outstretched hand
and sleeping under the mild stars,
flank to flank,
what did they do on freezing nights?
Still ignorant of nests and lairs
did they try to warm themselves
at the fiery leaves of the first autumn?

And how did they learn to sharpen
fangs and claws? Who taught them
the first lesson: that flesh
had been transformed to meat?
Tiger and Bear. Elk and Dove.
God saved them places on the Ark,
and Christ would honor them with
parables, calling himself the Lamb of God.

We train our dogs in strict obedience
at which we failed ourselves.
But sometimes the sound of barking
fills the night like distant artillery,

a sound as chilling as the bellow
of steers led up the ramps
of cattle cars whose gates swing
shut on them, as Eden's did.

from The Imperfect Paradise

SEASONAL

Which season is the loveliest of all?
Without a pause you smile and answer spring,
Thinking of Eden long before the fall.
I see green shrouds enclosing everything
And choose instead the chaos of the snow
Before God separated dark from light.
I hear the particles of matter blow
Through wintry landscapes on a wintry night.
You find the world a warm and charming place,
My Adam, you name everything in sight.
I find a garden of conspicuous waste—
The apple's flesh is cold and hard and white.
Still, at your touch my house warms to the eaves
As autumn torches all the fragile leaves.

IN THE GARDEN

How do we tell the flowers from the weeds
Now that the old equality of space
Has ended in the garden, and the seeds
Of milkweed and daisy scatter in disgrace?
Is it the stamen, petal, or the leaf
That like the ancient signature of Cain
Marks the flesh of wildflowers, to their grief
Just as the orchid blossoms into fame?
And Esau was the wildflower of his clan,
And Jacob was the brother who was chosen.
So we learn to distinguish man from man
Like botanists, our categories frozen.
But in a single morning roses die
While dandelions and chokeweed multiply.

THE IMPERFECT PARADISE

If God had stopped work after the fifth day
With Eden full of vegetables and fruits,
If oak and lilac held exclusive sway
Over a kingdom made of stems and roots,
If landscape were the genius of creation
And neither man nor serpent played a role
And God must look to wind for lamentation
And not to picture postcards of the soul,
Would he have rested on his bank of cloud
With nothing in the universe to lose,
Or would he hunger for a human crowd?
Which would a wise and just creator choose:
The green hosannas of a budding leaf
Or the strict contract between love and grief?

SOMEWHERE IN THE EUPHRATES

Somewhere in the Euphrates, buried, lost
The rusted gates of Eden still remain,
And archaeologists at awful cost
Search for a snakeskin or an apple stain,
Talk of Atlantis and the walls of Troy
As if they had to prove each legend real
Or else, like fools of science, must destroy
Geographies of what we only feel.
While sometimes watching at the window here
I see you in the garden on your knees;
It is as close as you have come to prayer,
Planting the shadblow and the peonies,
Making azaleas, hollies, dogwoods grow,
Digging up Eden with a single hoe.

from

HEROES IN DISGUISE,

1991

◆

Autumn

I want to mention
summer ending
without meaning the death
of somebody loved

or even the death
of the trees.
Today in the market
I heard a mother say

Look at the pumpkins,
it's finally autumn!
And the child didn't think
of the death of her mother

which is due before her own
but tasted the sound
of the words on her clumsy tongue:
pumpkin; autumn.

Let the eye enlarge
with all it beholds.
I want to celebrate
color, how one red leaf

flickers like a match
held to a dry branch,
and the whole world goes up
in orange and gold.

The Way the Leaves Keep Falling

It is November
and morning—time to get to work.
I feel the little whip
of my conscience flick
as I stand at the window watching
the great harvest of leaves.
Across the street my neighbor,
his leaf blower already roaring,
tries to make order
from the chaos of fading color.
He seems brave and a bit foolish.
It is almost tidal, the way
the leaves keep falling
wave after wave to earth.

In Eden there were
no seasons, and sometimes
I think it was the tidiness
of that garden
Eve hated, all the wooden tags
with the new names of plants and trees.
Still, I am Adam's child too
and I like order, though
the margins of my poems
are ragged, and I stand here
all morning watching the leaves.

The Myth of Perfectability

I hang the still life of flowers
by a window so it can receive
the morning light, as flowers must.
But sun will fade the paint,
so I move the picture to the exact center
of a dark wall, over the mantel
where it looks too much like a trophy—
one of those animal heads
but made up of blossoms.
I move it again to a little wall
down a hallway where I can come upon it
almost by chance, the way the Japanese
put a small window in an obscure place,
hoping that the sight of a particular landscape
will startle them with beauty as they pass
and not become familiar.
I do this all day long, moving
the picture or sometimes a chair or a vase
from place to place. Or else
I sit here at the typewriter,
putting in a comma to slow down
a long sentence, then taking it out,
then putting it back again
until I feel like a happy Sisyphus,
or like a good farmer who knows
that the body's work is never over,
for the motions of plowing and planting continue
season after season, even in his sleep.

Sculpture Garden

Between a bronze turtle
and a stone bird,
the wooden Adam and Eve,
carved with a chainsaw
out of old telephone poles,
stand sap-stained
in this flowerless garden,
ringed with the years
of the trees they came from
transformations ago.

I wonder if they remember
their lost leaves or the voices
that flew swifter than starlings
from telephone pole to telephone pole,
those cruciform shapes
lining the hills of the country
like stations of the cross.
It is early November.
This silence
between fall and winter

will be brief as the pause
between movements of music
when we listen
with all our attention
but may not applaud.
I think of the voices lost
since last winter. Sometimes
loneliness is so palpable
it becomes a presence
of its own, a kind of company.

Eden is lost
each time a child slides

through the torn gates
of its mother's thighs.
But here in an invented garden
I find a bestiary waiting
to be named: a wire cobra;
a turtle patient as bronze;
the stone wings of a bird
ready to fly.

The Bookstall

Just looking at them
I grow greedy, as if they were
freshly baked loaves
waiting on their shelves
to be broken open—that one
and that—and I make my choice
in a mood of exalted luck,
browsing among them
like a cow in sweetest pasture.

For life is continuous
as long as they wait
to be read—these inked paths
opening into the future, page
after page, every book
its own receding horizon.
And I hold them, one in each hand,
a curious ballast weighting me
here to the earth.

On the Marginality of Poets

At the margin of the pond,
in the live mud, there are frogs
whose whole bodies pulse,
the way the vein above
my father's eye pulsed
in thought. There are herons here,
the blue shape of flight, and small fish
whose blind seeking once
delivered all of us to land.

And on the margins of the page
it is all snow, no footfall yet.
Here is a perfect white frame
for anything, a place
where the sudden afterthought
is scrawled, or that brief star,
the asterisk. I want to live
in the margins:
those spaces neither here

nor there, like the crack
between my parents' pushed-together beds
where I used to lie; or the verge
of land between the meadow
and the woods, smooth
as the curve where a woman's
thigh and body join—
a path to the cave where life begins;
a place to watch from.

A New Poet

Finding a new poet
is like finding a new wildflower
out in the woods. You don't see

its name in the flower books, and
nobody you tell believes
in its odd color or the way

its leaves grow in splayed rows
down the whole length of the page. In fact
the very page smells of spilled

red wine and the mustiness of the sea
on a foggy day—the odor of truth
and of lying.

And the words are so familiar,
so strangely new, words
you almost wrote yourself, if only

in your dream there had been a pencil
or a pen or even a paintbrush,
if only there had been a flower.

Lost Luggage

"Dr. Magherini insists certain men and women
are susceptible to swooning in the presence
of great art, especially when far from home."

—*International New York Times*

Today in a palace disguised
as a museum, disguised myself
as a tourist, I entered a crucifixion scene
as part of the crowd and woke with the smell
of ancient sweat in my nostrils,
a bloody membrane over my eyes
as if I were seeing the world
through a crimson handkerchief—
they tell me I fainted.

Although I am in transit from my life,
I packed stray bits of it to take along—a comb
with relics of my greying hair, snapshots
of my own recent dead, books as thumbed
as this Bible chained to the hotel bedpost, whose verses
I read to put myself to sleep. At night
in different beds I dream of home,
but in the morning the dreams
are gone like so much lost luggage.

I know there are landscapes waiting
to be entered: forests shaded in leaf green
where winged children play on pipes;
the blue translucent scales of water in seascapes.
And on every wall are faces, gazing
through an undertow of brush strokes.
Meanwhile, framed in the evening windows
of yet another city, the woman reflected
is merely myself, the halo

of light a streetlamp shining on my head.
But ghosts clothed in tempera
follow me everywhere,
as if art itself were a purpling shadow
whose territory I must step back into,
a place where I can hide myself
over and over again, where what is lost
may be found, though always
in another language and untranslatable.

Unveiling

In the cemetery
a mile away
from where we used to live,
my aunts and mother
my father and uncles lie
in two long rows,
almost the way
they used to sit around
the long planked table
at family dinners.
And walking beside
the graves today, down
one straight path
and up the next,
I don't feel sad, exactly,
just left out a bit,
as if they kept
from me the kind
of grown-up secret
they used to share
back then, something
I'm not quite ready yet
to learn.

Subway

Sometimes at night
I put myself
to sleep
with the names
of subway stops
between 125th
and Fordham Road: 134th . . .
145th . . . 161st . . .
The tunnel unwinds
backwards
under ruined streets
towards a room
where my mother sits
and mediates
between my need
and my father's
silence.
Childhood is cold
comfort.
The subway roars
and shakes—memory's
beast—over
its slippery tracks:
167th . . . 174th . . .
and I cling
to the loop
of numbers
as if I had an appointment
to keep,
as if my mother
and father were not
somewhere else
underground,
already asleep.

An Old Song

How loyal our childhood demons are,
growing old with us in the same house
like servants who season the meat
with bitterness, like jailers
who rattle the keys
that lock us in or lock us out.

Though we go on with our lives,
though the years pile up
like snow against the door,
still our demons stare at us
from the depths of mirrors
or from the new faces across a table.

And no matter what voice they choose,
what language they speak,
the message is always the same.
They ask "Why can't you do
anything right?" They say
"We just don't love you anymore."

The Hat Lady

In a childhood of hats—
my uncles in homburgs and derbies,
Fred Astaire in high black silk,
the yarmulke my grandfather wore
like the palm of a hand
cradling the back of his head—
only my father went hatless,
even in winter.

And in the spring,
when a turban of leaves appeared
on every tree, the Hat Lady came
with a fan of pins in her mouth
and pins in her sleeves,
the Hat Lady came—
that Saint Sebastian of pins,
to measure my mother's head.

I remember a hat of dove grey felt
that settled like a bird
on the nest of my mother's hair.
I remember a pillbox that tilted
over one eye—pure Myrna Loy,
and a navy straw with cherries caught
at the brim that seemed real enough
for a child to have to pick.

Last year when the chemicals
took my mother's hair, she wrapped
a towel around her head. And the Hat Lady came,
a bracelet of needles on each arm,
and led her to a place
where my father and grandfather waited,
head to bare head, and Death
winked at her and tipped his cap.

Cousins

We meet at funerals
every few years—another star
in the constellation of our family
put out—and even in that failing
light, we look completely
different, completely the same.
"What are you doing now?"
we ask each other, "How
have you been?" At these times
the past is more palpable
than our children waiting
at home or the wives and husbands tugging
at our sleeves. "Remember . . . ?"
we ask, "Remember the time . . . ?"
And laughter is as painful
as if our ribs had secret
cracks in them.
Our childhoods remain
only in the sharp bones
of our noses, the shape
of our eyes, the way our genes call out
to each other in the high-pitched notes
that only kin can hear.
How much of memory
is imagination? And if loss
is an absence, why does it grow
so heavy? These are the questions
we mean when we ask: "Where
are you living now?" or
"How old is your youngest?"
Sometimes I feel the grief
of these occasions swell
in me until I become
an instrument in which language rises
like music. But all

that the others can hear
is my strangled voice calling
"Goodbye . . . " calling
"Keep in touch . . . "
with the kind of sound
a bagpipe makes, its bellows heaving,
and even its marching music funereal.

Angels

"Are you tired of angels?"

—MYRA SKLAREW

I am tired of angels,
of how their great wings
rustle open the way a curtain opens
on a play I have no wish to see.
I am tired of their milky robes,
their star-infested sashes,
of their perfect fingernails
translucent as shells
from which the souls
of tiny creatures have already fled.

Remember Lucifer, I want to tell them,
his crumpled bat wings
nose-diving from grace.
But they would simply laugh
with the watery sound a harp makes
cascading through bars of music.
Or they would sing to me in
my mother's lost voice,
extracting all the promises
I made to her but couldn't keep.

1932—

I saw my name in print the other day
with 1932 and then a blank
and knew that even now some grassy bank
just waited for my grave. And somewhere a grey

slab of marble existed already
on which the final number would be carved—
as if the stone itself were somehow starved
for definition. When I went steady

in high school years ago, my boyfriend's name
was what I tried out, hearing how it fit
with mine; then names of film stars in some hit.
My husband was anonymous as rain.

There is a number out there, odd or even
that will become familiar to my sons
and daughter. (They are the living ones
I think of now: Peter, Rachel, Stephen.)

I picture it, four integers in a row
5 or 7, 6 or 2 or 9:
a period; silence; an end-stopped line;
a hammer poised . . . delivering its blow.

The Happiest Day

It was early May, I think
a moment of lilac or dogwood
when so many promises are made
it hardly matters if a few are broken.
My mother and father still hovered
in the background, part of the scenery
like the houses I had grown up in,
and if they would be torn down later
that was something I knew
but didn't believe. Our children were asleep
or playing, the youngest as new
as the new smell of the lilacs,
and how could I have guessed
their roots were shallow
and would be easily transplanted.
I didn't even guess that I was happy.
The small irritations that are like salt
on melon were what I dwelt on,
though in truth they simply
made the fruit taste sweeter.
So we sat on the porch
in the cool morning, sipping
hot coffee. Behind the news of the day—
strikes and small wars, a fire somewhere—
I could see the top of your dark head
and thought not of public conflagrations
but of how it would feel on my bare shoulder.
If someone could stop the camera then . . .
if someone could only stop the camera
and ask me: are you happy?
perhaps I would have noticed
how the morning shone in the reflected
color of lilac. Yes, I might have said
and offered a steaming cup of coffee.

Balance

On the small, imaginary
kitchen scales,
I place on one side
all the scraps memory
has left me, as if I could make
a meal of them;
and on the other, all
I can surmise of the indelible
future: anniversaries,
losses. On one side I place
my mother's suede glove—
that emptied udder;

on the other the mitten
my grandson just dropped—
a woolen signpost he'll soon
outgrow. He is three;
she has been gone three years
exactly. Equilibrium is simply
that moment when the present
is as real as the past
or the future, when the air
that nourishes us
we breathe
without thinking.

March 27

In this country
it snows one day
and summer comes the next,
there are no boundaries
green spreads unchecked
and under last year's leaves
the newly living and the dead
consort, as on those canvasses
of Judgement Day when weather
is finished and if God had a purpose
to his seasons, all the flowers
of heaven must answer to it.

Crocuses

They come
by stealth, spreading
the rumor of spring—
near the hedge . . .
by the gate . . .
at our chilly feet . . .
mothers of saffron, fathers
of insurrection, purple
and yellow scouts
of an army still massing
just to the south.

Misreading Housman

On this first day of spring, snow
covers the fruit trees, mingling improbably
with the new blossoms like identical twins
brought up in different hemispheres.
It is not what Housman meant
when he wrote of the cherry
hung with snow, though he also knew
how death can mistake the seasons,
and if he made it all sound pretty,
that was our misreading
in those high school classrooms
where, drunk on boredom, we had to recite
his poems. Now the weather is always looming

in the background, trying to become more
than merely scenery, and though today
it is telling us something
we don't want to hear, it is all
so unpredictable, so out of control
that we might as well be children again,
hearing the voices of thunder
like baritone uncles shouting
in the next room as we try to sleep,
or hearing the silence of snow falling
soft as a coverlet, even in springtime
whispering: relax, there is nothing
you can possibly do about any of this.

Gleaning

Driving from coast
to coast down looped highways,
I notice how the future
we have been speeding towards for years
is receding behind us.
We must have crossed some boundary

and hardly noticed; people
we once hurried to greet
are standing along the roadside
waving goodbye, your grandfather
in his ancestral cap, my mother
holding aloft a flowered hanky.

Still we travel on,
the car radio playing music
we danced to
how many years ago?
When I try to count
I put myself to sleep.

"Talk to me," you say, "don't
doze off." We must watch for
whatever the stubborn flesh
still offers: the smell of hay
sharp and sweet on the air,
desire—that old song.

Look out the car window.
Hogs have been let loose
in the stubbled fields
like heroes in disguise
to find what grains of corn
are left.

from
AN EARLY AFTERLIFE,
1995

◆

The Python

The children holding the python
all along its ten-foot mottled body
are like the blind men with the elephant—
what can they know
of what they hold beneath their fingers,
these not quite babies
still in the Eden of preschool,
sloughing off their winter jackets now
in the steamy weather
of the reptile house.

And this creature they dare
to carry, this undulating river
of muscle, supple and curving and
thick as the arm of its keeper,
what does it know of sin
or apples, wanting only to follow the flick
of its two-pronged tongue
(like those blind men following
their tapping canes) to anyplace
its hunger takes it.

The Lumberjacks

They entered Eden
with their saws and axes,
and as Eve watched
from just beyond the gate
they turned the live trees
into timber, a carnage

of chestnut, cedar, alder,
spilling the fruit and
stripping the bark, measuring,
cutting into four-by-fours and
two-by-sixes—numbering
now instead of naming, until

even the complicitous apple
was felled, and the smell
of sawdust was like death
in the nostrils,
and it was evening
and another day.

Espaliered Pear Trees

You tack the pear trees to the wall
in a mime of crucifixion—
their limbs splayed flat,
their leafed backs toward us—
and water them with a hose.

Last week you called the bonsai
living haiku, paring
its tender branches
as ruthlessly
as you would your nails,

while I could only think
of Chinese women
tottering
on their bound feet.
Here in the garden,

where the cost of beauty
is partly pain, we kneel
on the resilient ground
trying to befriend the soil
we must become.

Long after Eden,
the imagination flourishes
with all its unruly weeds.
I dream of the fleeting
taste of pears.

The Book

In the book of shadows
the first page is dark
and the second darker still,
but on the next page,
and the next, there is a flickering
as if the shadows are dancing
with themselves, as if they are dancing
with the leaves they mimic.
Before Narcissus found the pool
it was his shadow he loved,

the way we grow to love our deaths
when we meet them
in dreams. For as we turn
the pages of the book
each page grows heavier
under our numbed fingers, and only
the shadows themselves
are weightless,
only the shadows welcome us
beneath their cool canopy.

Narcissus at 60

If love hadn't made him clumsy,
if he hadn't fallen forward,
had never drowned
in his own perfection,

what would he have thought
about his aging face
as it altered, year after year
season by season?

In the old conspiracy
between the eye
and its reflection, love casts
a primal shadow.

Perhaps he would blame
the wrinkling surface of the pool
for what he saw
or think the blemishes

on his once smooth cheek
were simply small fish
just beneath the lethal skin
of the water.

At Indian River Inlet

Long before there was light, water
existed, as if chaos itself
had been a kind of rainstorm.

Maybe that's why this landscape seems
so elemental, a place
where blues and greens leak

into each other, where water
and land are married
with all the binding ties of salt.

Today the wind moves
over the flat plain of the cove,
bending the waves

into rows. I could be standing
in a field somewhere
watching

the grass blades bow, regiment
by regiment,
as far as the horizon.

Even the single fisherman
leaning over the side
of his boat

is like some good farmer, seeding
the water with prayers
and curses, setting his bait

with a love based upon hunger,
a skepticism only the faithful
really know.

Our own tides move restlessly
in and out. Color rushes
to our faces, then subsides,

love comes and goes,
tears in their mercy catch
at our reedy lashes. At night

our houses sink
on their foundations
like small boats rocking on their heels,

and over creek and estuary,
field and farm,
over every ambiguity

of darkness
the moon comes, casting
its mended net.

Ideal City

oil on panel, Central Italy, c.1500

Set in the silence of pure perspective,
the ideal city has no people in it,
only buildings. On these streets Order rules
with a golden stylus, and in the balance
of dome and arch and doorframe, we find
serenity, child of proportion.
Maybe this place is an alternate Eden
created by an urban God who hated gardens.
Or maybe this is Heaven just before Judgement Day,
and the buildings are simply waiting for the Chosen
who will rise from their graves to come and inhabit them.
At night when the clarity of light must finally fade
I hope that the Virtues step down from their columns to dance
a little or, better still, cook pasta in the invisible kitchens.

But the Italian clouds with their casual cumulus shapes
don't really belong in this sky, and though the doorways
are partly ajar, they seem to open on nothing but blankness.
In such a city, I wonder where lovers can embrace
or where the dog can lift his shaggy leg.
Then I want to break all the laws of Geometry,
to litter these spotless streets with the pungency
of orange peels and the glaze of cigarette wrappers,
to put my arms around the bronzed columns, then shinny
up them, pretending to be one of the Virtues myself.
I want to run through the streets playing the radio
with its volume turned all the way up.
I want to sign my name, and yours,
with the scarlet graffiti of laughter.

Camping at the Headlands of the Rappahannock

We love each landscape
as if it were a part
of our human body,

even the desert
with its waterless beaches;
even the craters of the moon—

those blistered rocks
we christen with the names
of our desire.

Limbs of trees we say,
or foothills,
or bodies of water,

and it is more than metaphor we mean
when we take the river
into our arms.

Agoraphobia

"Yesterday the bird of night did sit,
Even at noon-day, upon the marketplace,
Hooting and shrieking."

—WILLIAM SHAKESPEARE

1.

Imagine waking
to a scene of snow so new
not even memories
of other snow
can mar its silken
surface. What other innocence
is quite like this,
and who can blame me
for refusing
to violate such whiteness
with the booted cruelty
of tracks?

2.

Though I cannot leave this house,
I have memorized the view
from every window—
23 framed landscapes, containing
each nuance of weather and light.
And I know the measure
of every room, not as a prisoner
pacing a cell
but as the embryo knows
the walls of the womb, free
to swim as its body tells it, to nudge
the softly fleshed walls,
dreading only the moment

of contraction when it will be forced
into the gaudy world.

3.

Sometimes I travel as far
as the last stone
of the path, but
every step,
as in the children's story,
pricks that tender place
on the bottom of the foot,
and like an ebbing tide with all
the obsession of the moon behind it,
I am dragged back.

4.

I have noticed in windy fall
how leaves are torn from the trees,
each leaf waving goodbye to the oak
or the poplar that housed it;
how the moon, pinned
to the very center of the window,
is like a moth wanting only to break in.
What I mean is this house
follows all the laws of lintel and ridgepole,
obeys the commandments of broom
and of needle, custom and grace.
It is not fear that holds me here but passion
and the uncrossable moat of moonlight
outside the bolted doors.

Smoke Screen

I love the many dialects of smoke,
leaf smoke and pipe smoke,
chimney smoke,
the way in spite of gravity
it always rises,
as if it were assembling
in some pungent niche of heaven.
I used to love the smoke rings
you blew, those insubstantial
lassos of desire
that roped me in.
Now I love woodsmoke
and kitchen smoke—the breath of soup
lifting from the pot, contrails
of morning toast, barely burning.
Consider the signals the Indians sent—
that first skywriting,
or how all fires give up the ghost
in veils, in clouds like parachutes
ascending. I love the way
from every household hearth
a genie spirals up a helix
of its own making.
And we walk home, watching
the smoke our breath makes
on the wintry air, not noticing
our days, our nights going slowly
up in smoke.

Stationary Bicycle

You pedal furiously
into a future you're trying
hard to prolong
by this exercise,
though the landscape
that rolls by here is time
passing, with its lists
of things undone
or not done properly,
and all this effort,
the fierce monotony
of this ride feels
much like life itself—
going nowhere
strenuously,
redeemed in part
by the imagination, its trance
of rivers and trees,
its shady roads unwinding
just beyond your closed eyes,
or even on the tv screen
you sometimes watch
as you ride, mile
after mile of drama
unfolding while you pump
and pump, proceeding
from here to here
at twenty theoretical
miles per hour, your legs
beginning to throb, as if
the body communicates
in a code of pain, saying
never mind the future,
you're here
right now, alive.

The English Novel

In The English Novel, where I spent my girlhood,
I used to think chilblains were a kind of biscuit,
and everything was always pearled with fog—
the moors with their purpling heather
and the bevelled windows where the heroines,
my sisters, waited for heroes
who would find them eventually, after one or both
threaded their way through some kind of moral
labyrinth, shadowed and thorny. He was worth waiting for,
and anyway the slowness of the clocks was deliberate
as if minutes, like pence, had different meanings then.
There was no polyester. Everything was brocade and velvet,
even the landscapes, those hills embroidered
with flowers, and though sex was hardly mentioned
it was clearly a scent in the air like the sachets
in the cupboards, subtle but pervasive as the smell
of lavender or viburnum or tallow from all the smoky,
snuffed-out candles. Furniture and forests, marriages
were eternal then, and though there was always a plot
it hardly mattered. As for too much coincidence,
doesn't the moon always wander through the sky at the exact
moment the lovers are wandering through the park, even today,
even in this city with its fake Victorian facades?
And all the familiar faces we notice at the movies
or across a restaurant, couldn't they be our half brothers
or cousins, lost once in the deep and mysterious gene pool—
descendants, some of them, of Emma and Mr. Knightly,
or the ones with Russian faces descended from Ladislaw maybe,
who could have come from a place just a few hours by carriage
from the shtetl where my great-great-grandmother
somehow acquired her blonde hair and blue, blue eyes?

the arithmetic of alternation

today I write
of the shadows
flowers make
on a white wall,
the texture of petals
and leaves like a flat braille,
a brightness
even without color

but tomorrow
I will tell
how on the warmest day
there is an icy edge
to things, a darkness
at the rim
of every shining
object

this is the arithmetic
of alternation,
the way the hours,
the seasons
arrange themselves,
it keeps us honest,
it keeps us turning
the page

The Bronx, 1942

When I told him to shut up,
my father slammed the brakes and left
me like a parcel in the car
on a strange street, to punish me
he said for lack of respect, though
what he always feared was lack of love.
I know now just how long

forgiveness can take
and that it can be harder than respect,
or even love. My father stayed angry
for a week. But I still remember
the gritty color of the sky through
that windshield and how, like a parcel,
I started to come apart.

Courbet's *Still Life with Apples and Pomegranate*

To lift himself from one of his depressions,
my father took up painting, oil on canvas
for which he had no teacher,
just an apprenticeship in sheer will
and bagfulls of groceries to practice on.

I can still smell those apples, and sometimes peaches,
going slyly to rot on my mother's velvet shawl
whose blue folds he slowly re-created
one by one by one as if they were waves
on an artificial ocean.

Courbet's fruit have so much roundness,
such warmth and homeliness beside the pewter tankard,
you could almost say they had humanity,
if apples could be human.
And as I stand in this crowded museum,

all these years after my father's death,
they make me grieve for him
and his precise, mistaken apples,
not for his failures;
for how stubbornly he tried.

High Summer

The earth smells of flowers
and corruption—so many
shades of green
that caterpillar and leaf
are indistinguishable,
even as one obliterates
the other.

Aunt Ruth sits
on the back porch, rocking
towards her death.
The smallest cousin swims
into the future. Look
at the water, so beautiful
in all that it conceals.

In a Northern Country

Yesterday in a northern country
my last aunt died, taking
my maiden name with her into silence,
and there is no one left
who knew her here
for me to tell.

I am tired of the litany
of months, September . . . October . . .
I am tired of the way the seasons
keep changing, mimicking
the seasons of the flesh
which are real and finite.

The world wounds us
with its beauty, as if it knew
we had to leave it soon.
She must have watched
the deep Canadian lake she loved
sheathe itself in early ice,

the few last leaves
on the birch tree tremble
like half notes, vibrato
outside her sickroom window
until November came
with its winds and took them.

Ghosts

My lovely ghosts are unaware
of boundaries. They step from my dreams
into the early morning air
as if they were offering
breakfast, the way they used to.

They have my sculpted cheekbones,
my severe hair. At dusk
I see them reflected
in the darkening windows
beyond which, like static

from a distant transmission,
the bitter snow is starting to fall.
Oh my lovely ghosts,
when I speak your names aloud
I think you forgive me.

Old Photograph Album

These pages, crumbling under my fingers
as I turn them, chronicle the lives
of the people I loved, years before
I was there to love them. Mother.
Great-aunts and cousins. Here are their naked
infancies on sheepskin rugs; their exodus
across decades of childhood and youth;
the shy solemnity of their weddings.
In the old country my father in knickers
clowns and spends his foreign dollars
on his last visit before that country
closes down. The Adirondacks.
The Catskills. New York—its pushcarts,
its ancient children—more foreign
to me than the streets of Troy or Rome.
The glue loosens under the small black
triangles that hold the pictures in place,
reminding me of those torn
pieces of mourning ribbon pinned
to our blouses or coats at funerals.
Here are the people I have lost
because I can't believe in the green
pastureland of hymns or in the haloed
faces of angels, outlined
in golden threads on altar cloths:
Grandma and Grandpa,
Ada, Leo, and Ruth. If only I thought
we would meet just one more time
even in purgatory, that anteroom
to someone else's heaven, with its horsehair sofas
and shabby twenties' furniture, peopled
with ghosts in high starched collars and velvet hats.

The Laws of Primogeniture

My grandson has my father's mouth
with its salty sayings
and my grandfather's crooked ear
which heard the soldiers coming.

He has the pale eyes of the cossack
who saw my great-great-grandmother
in the woods, then wouldn't stop
looking.

And see him now, pushing
his bright red firetruck towards
a future he thinks he's inventing
all by himself.

What We Fear Most
for R after the accident

We have been saved one more time
from what we fear most.
Let us remember this moment.
Let us forget it if we can.
Just now a kind of golden dust
settles over everything:
the tree outside the window,
though it is not fall;
the cracked sugar bowl,
so carefully mended once.
This light is not redemption,
just the silt of afternoon sun
on an ordinary day,
unlike any other.

Flowers

Someone I love is getting married,
and I am composing poems about flowers, hyacinths
and lilacs, as if there were something
intrinsically bridal about these outgrowths of the plant
flaunting itself, attracting insects and birds
to the exact and fragrant place of pollen.

And someone I love is dying.
Flowers will be wanted for her too,
lilies perhaps, though all that is required
is a handful of good dirt on a plain pine box,
and all the funeral bouquets will be sent
to a hospital somewhere, where the sick will wake

one morning to a confusion of scents.
I wonder, partly in innocence,
why everything seems to mean something else,
and I marvel at how we comfort
ourselves and each other with the fragile
symptoms of beauty, with petals

of roses for love, with snowdrops for hope,
whether we are setting out on a journey
or simply waving goodbye from the dock
as the ship pulls out and a wake of tossed flowers
floats for a little while, delicate as foam
on the water, before it disappears.

Snow Showers, a Prothalamion

for Rachel and David

You are teaching my daughter the language
of the stars, the whole sky
glazed with them in freezing Wisconsin,
and both your faces tilted up
as though you were reading, were trying
to learn by heart the night's
illuminated pages. I picture her
putting her eye to a telescope and seeing
her first close-up
of what I still call the heavens.
It must have been like seeing a man's face (yours)
stubbled and cratered, an eyelash length away.
She was a most inventive child.
Now she gives the spin of reality
to her made-up worlds,

while you, fledgling astronomer,
make real worlds with their long itineraries of light
seem touched with phantasy.
I want to tell you both how a moment ago
there were snow showers here,
though the sun is back now, and the grass
remains a frozen, spiky green.
But just a moment ago the sky seemed to release
entire galaxies, and stars or star-shaped flakes,
whatever that charged and bridal whiteness was,
swarmed at the windows
until the real and the imagined
became one, a perfect marriage
of opposites, like mine has been.
Come spring, like yours.

Vermilion

Pierre Bonnard would enter
the museum with a tube of paint
in his pocket and a sable brush.
Then violating the sanctity
of one of his own frames
he'd add a stroke of vermilion
to the skin of a flower.
Just so I stopped you
at the door this morning
and licking my index finger, removed
an invisible crumb
from your vermilion mouth. As if
at the ritual moment of departure
I had to show you still belonged to me.
As if revision were
the purest form of love.

Foreshadowing

is what writers call it, meaning
Chekov's famous pistol
which must go off in the final act;
or how an aging poet used melancholy
as the alphabet of childhood.

It is the hint God gave us
when He invented night
on the first page of creation—
a recurring darkness over Eden
long before the fall.

It is one red leaf in August;
a wrinkled newborn's
sharp, protesting cry.
I remember our first kiss, the way
it went on and on as if we knew

to separate even once would be dangerous,
would foreshadow a final
parting, real as a gunshot
which, mouth against mouth,
we could deny.

The Apple Shrine

Last week you gathered armfuls of apple blossoms
from trees along the roadway, and a few
from the bent Cortland down the street
to place beneath our nameless apple tree
for pollination, you said, so we'd have fruit
next winter. Looking out the window at those rags
and shreds of blossoms beneath the tree,
it could have been a makeshift shrine I saw
in one of those unlikely places where miracles
are said to happen, sightings of angels
or the Virgin, where later ordinary people
place gifts of dolls and colored handkerchiefs.
How fitting, I thought, as if we worshiped
the garden itself, or spring. Just one day later
and equally strange, but fearful

you seemed to lose your vision, went half blind
after work in the garden, for a transgression
not even you with your Science understand.
Healing too is mysterious, the way the seasons
heal each other, one month at a time;
or what can happen in a week in a darkened room
where we both sat thinking about how quickly
everything can change, how thin the crust
of ice we walk on—such thoughts themselves perhaps
a kind of prayer. Today you start to see again,
and I wonder how long we'll remember to be grateful
before we lose ourselves complicitously
in the everyday, waking up surprised one morning
next autumn when for the first time
our tree will be strung with a rosary of apples.

Hardwood

Do these gnarled and twisted trees
feel greenness surge
at their roots the way saplings do?
When a new leaf breaks through
are they astonished,
as Sarah must have been,
at such an improbable birth?

The woodpecker, with its
firing squad rat-tat-tat, knows
each vulnerable spot on the wrinkled bark.
In a month these trees will resurrect
a shade to sit beneath.
There are stumps
to rest on everywhere.

Sometimes

from the periphery
of the family
where I sit watching
my children and
my children's children
in all their bright
cacophony,

I seem to leave
my body—
plump effigy
of a woman, upright
on a chair—
and as I float
willingly away

toward the chill
silence of my own future,
their voices break
into the syllables
of strangers, to whom
with this real hand
I wave goodbye.

An Early Afterlife

"... a wise man in time of peace, shall
make the necessary preparations for war."

—HORACE

Why don't we say goodbye right now
in the fallacy of perfect health
before whatever is going to happen
happens. We could perfect our parting,
like those characters in *On the Beach*
who said farewell in the shadow
of the bomb as we sat watching,
young and holding hands at the movies.
We could use the loving words
we otherwise might not have time to say.
We could hold each other for hours
in a quintessential dress rehearsal.

Then we would just continue
for however many years were left.
The ragged things that are coming next—
arteries closing like rivers silting over,
or rampant cells stampeding us to the exit—
would be like postscripts to our lives
and wouldn't matter. And we would bask
in an early afterlife of ordinary days,
impervious to the inclement weather
already in our long-range forecast.
Nothing could touch us. We'd never
have to say goodbye again.

Index of Titles and First Lines